THE STREETS CALL ME TREASURE 2

This is a work of fiction. All of the characters, names, places, organizations, and events portrayed in this novel are either products of the author's imagination or are used fictitiously. Any resemblance to actual events or locales or persons, living or dead, is entirely coincidental.

The Streets Call Me Treasure 2 Copyright ©2016 by Shaunta Kenerly.

All rights reserved. Printed in the United States of America. No part of this book may be used or reproduced in any form or by any means without written consent except in the case of brief quotations embodied in critical articles or reviews.

ISBN-13: 978-0692659977

ISBN-10: 0692659978

Publisher:

kenerlypresents.com

shauntakenerlypresents@gmail.com

Facebook: Shaunta Kenerly/Kenerly Publishing fan page

Charlotte, N.C.

First Edition: February 2016

10 9 8 7 6 5 4 3 2 1

Editors: Annetta Gabrielle Hobson

Cover Design: Muneca Smith

Printed in the United States of America

THE STREETS CALL ME TREASURE 2
The Art of Seduction

SHAUNTA KENERLY

KENERLY PRESENTS PUBLICATION

CHAPTER 1

Brian thought he had a trick up his sleeve taking me out on a shopping spree today. He even had someone take my car out to get detailed, knowing how much I hated taking the car to a shop to get cleaned. Bruthas were always thirsty trying to get a taste of this pussy. I wouldn't give them the time of day. Sometimes they would try to flash some money or stunt in their European whips; but if they had only known that I was the chic to take all of their hard earned dope money. The huge rock on my hand seemed like it only attracted the worst of them. Most men didn't care if I said I was happily married with a ten-year-old son. That line was like an open invitation to try harder. The fact that he did listen to my complaining multiple times earned him some pussy points.

Brian's artists accidently slipped up bragging about a label tour two days ago. They were in the studio, smoking and drinking with some dusty ass girls bragging about their upcoming tour. Soon as the word "tour" rolled off of one of the artist's tongue, I busted into the studio raising hell. I played it off like I was mad about the half-naked women lying around but I wanted them to leave so I could get the 411 on this tour. Brian was acting weird lately and I knew that he was hiding something.

The artists tried to resist revealing the details but I managed to threaten them with lack of studio time. They wasn't about to play with that, since they both had albums they were working to finish. The engineer looked up at me and quickly turned his head knowing that I wasn't playing. They began to talk like old ladies. I knew what cities they were going to perform, the dates, and more importantly if Brian was attending the tour. I only had one rule when he hit the road and that was no hoes on the tour bus. I knew how men were easily persuaded by a cute face, fat ass, and wet pussy.

After they spilled the beans, I exited the studio and made plans of my own. I changed into my new two-piece swimming suit. Brian wasn't home to complain, so I decided to throw it on. I went to the backyard and relaxed in the pool. I sat in the pool thinking about the guy whom I was going to rob. I met him at a jewelry store near the Polaris mall. I was getting my rings cleaned and he came in to buy some jewelry for himself. He tried to persuade me with the purchase of a bracelet but I denied him without hesitation. That must have drove him crazy. Before I could turn to leave the store, he grabbed my wrist and begged for me to call him. He said that same ole bullshit about going out to eat but honestly I knew what he wanted to eat. I gave him a gentle smile as I took his number. I promised to visit him soon and that made his day. When I finally broke his grasp he gave me a slap on the ass and reminded me to call him.

Although Brian had given me everything I wanted, I just wanted things for myself. I didn't feel right using his money to buy him things. I wasn't a bum bitch. The money that I made from the dance studio barely took care of the bills for the studio. I was always helping out young dancers whose family didn't have the money to pay for outfits and classes. I also paid my dance instructors a very competitive wage for their contribution. Any monies left over I used on the house or Raymond.

With Brian's birthday only a week away, I wanted to do it big for him. Brian was turning the big "30" and he was going to truly enjoy it. I planned on taking a trip to Las Vegas for the entire week of his birthday and anything he wanted he could have. I already invited Anna, an instructor from my dance school, to join us. She was delighted with the invitation of joining us in Vegas. Shit I was delighted with the thought of having her there.

Anna was a single twenty-three-year old Black and Asian woman. She was more Black than she was Asian. Her facial features, such as her eyes and nose, showed her Asian genetics; but her lips, hips, breast and ass, definitely came from her momma (not to mention her sassy attitude.) The girl was perfectly built. Her body shaped well in her latex pants and sports bra revealing her pierced navel. The girl had a six pack to die for. Her breasts were full and plump. Her ass was the same size as mine but firm from constant exercise. Anna made the other female instructors jealous. They often tried to get me to fire her saying that she was dressing too sexy for class or claimed that she was in the parking-lot flirting with a student's father. They were all lies. The ladies were just behaving like jealous fools because she was a bad chic.

About two months earlier, I found out that Anna was into me when she asked to touch my ass after I bent over to slip on my heels. She was standing behind me admiring my ass like a man would. She wanted to know if my ass was real and after I told her numerous of times that it was 100% real she insisted on touching it. I allowed her to touch it and her hands slid from my ass to my breast. I stared into her eyes as she caressed my body. Her hands continued to caress my body until they found my sweet spot. I sat on the edge of my desk knocking off the pictures of Brian and Raymond onto the floor. She tugged away at my pants until she had thrown them against the floor. She didn't waste any time taking her tongue and gliding it up and down my pussy. I held her jet black hair in my hands and assisted her head where I wanted

THE STREETS CALL ME TREASURE 2

her to concentrate on. The girl was trying her hardest to make me cum but I just couldn't. I mean she stuck her fingers inside of me and thrusted in and out. She sucked on my clit passionately. She licked on my pussy lips moaning and making my pussy wetter but I just couldn't cum. Anna knew it was a problem. She stopped and glared at me with a puppy dog look and I had to explain to her that I really wasn't into females after the last experience I had with a woman. She tried to understand but I knew she thought that she was the problem.

Ever since that day she has been taunting me to have sex with her. She promised that she would allow me to do with her as I would. So weeks after she tasted my pussy, I got her alone in the office again and this time I was the aggressor. I pulled her shirt off and sucked on her breast getting her all aroused. I had her light brown nipples in my mouth licking on each of them in a circular motion. I kissed her passionately sucking on her lips and while I held her ass firmly. I planted kisses from her breast down to her navel simultaneously massaging her clit. Then I just stopped. Anna was out of breath. She struggled to ask why but I just walked away. Anna began to cry. I told her to come to me. She placed her face on my lap and just cried. I told her that the only way we could do this was to include my husband. I didn't want her fucking him but if I had a change of heart, he wasn't going in her raw. I'd be damn if he would give another woman a baby before he gave me one. She was going to be our play toy. I told her about our week long getaway to Vegas and she was with it. I bought her plane tickets and the party was in motion.

Brian deserved a special birthday party and I was going to give him one with my own money. I had to lick this guy for whatever he had in order to get Brian everything that I wanted him to have. Besides the trip to Vegas and an extra body for his pleasure, I planned on buying him a new Rolex and this old school car we saw for sale. The dance school money wasn't going to do it so I knew what had to be done.

Knowing that the guy was from Cleveland, I had to do my homework. The bruthas up there were just like the bruthas back at home in Dayton; grimy, hustlers, go getters, body baggers. I had to be careful or I could possibly be sent back home with a toe tag.

I made the two hour trip up to Cleveland every weekend. I found out where he hung out and even followed him to his baby momma's house. His baby momma greeted him at the door with their young son. The boy looked just like his father. His baby momma was flawless. Her milk chocolate skin didn't have any blemishes. Her skin was hypnotizing; looking as if she worked for Cover Girl or was a Jet Beauty of The Week. Although her tone was dark, it shimmered in the light. She wore a glow around her. Money would try to enter the house but she kept him right on the porch like a stray dog. She allowed him to see their son on the front porch. Money would play with him for a few minutes then ride off.

The streets were talking so I knew that he was getting rid of ten to twenty bricks of heroin a week. He was the perfect lick. The bad part was that he was fine as hell but this was business only. I hadn't hit a lick in years and he was the perfect target. He wouldn't even expect the robbery from me when he was out here flaunting his money around like a celebrity.

When we finally walked out of the mall, Brian confessed the news in which I had already knew. He was looking so bashful and nervous. I found it to be cute. He was worried to death about my reaction to his news.

"Baby, I am going on tour with the whole label. I will be back soon after we come back from our show in Louisville then ending in Cleveland. We have those cities back to back."

"Cleveland?" I said curiously.

"Yeah Cleveland!"

"Okay. Well, call every time you get a chance."

"You know that I will."

"Brian your birthday is a week away," I said trying to sound sad.

"I know. I will be back home before then. It's only a three city tour and we will only be gone for four days," he answered.

"Okay because I have some big plans for us. I want you to tell your assistant to clear your schedule the whole week of your birthday."

"Damn! You don't want to celebrate The Fourth of July here? You know how much you love the fireworks."

"Oh we will have some fireworks alright."

We both laughed.

Brian and I continued to have a good evening. He took me to a nice restaurant and we had a table set outside all alone. The weather was just right to eat outside and enjoy each other's company. The waiter had wine on chill and the candles lit for the perfect ambiance. I was fighting hard to show my true feelings of joy because I was upset about not being dressed for the occasion. Brian was a real good man. He kept me on my toes. Just when I thought that I knew the man he would surprise me again.

CHAPTER 2

With Brian gone on tour with his music artists, I decided that now would be the perfect time to reach out to Money, the hustler, from Cleveland. I was already on interstate 71 before I made the call. I was going to make sure that I saw him regardless of what he was going to say. I was either going to catch him slipping, out kicking it and follow him home, or we were going to meet up like he had planned. I gave myself three days to rob him.

Money was surprised to hear from me. He thought that I was some stuck up bitch. He claimed that most Columbus girls that he had ran into was stuck up. I played things off like I was excited to see him. I told him that I had some college friends staying up there and I was coming to visit them but I wanted to see him while I was there. He took the bait. Money said that he had floor seats to the Cav's playoff game tonight and if I was interested, he would like for me to join him. I pretended to be excited and said yes. He thought he had me, but it was the other way around.

Money picked me up three hours after I checked into my hotel. That gave me just enough time to get dressed and put my make-up on. I already had my hair and nails done so all that was left was to capture the man with his first glance. I picked out the perfect pair of jeans to show off my curves and a top showing nothing but cleavage. I sprayed myself with some body spray and rushed down to his car.

Money had a white on white 2014 Challenger. White paint. White rims. White interior. The car was nice; I must admit. On the side of the car it read 'Got Milk.' I managed to let my guard down and giggle. The sign was very creative, it only spoke out on his personality. When he saw me, he immediately climbed out and opened the passenger door like a gentleman. I was surprised by this action because when we first met, he was just like all of the other men that were trying to get inside of my panties.

Money started the conversation with asking me about my trip up here. He wondered if I was well rested enough to sit through a whole game. I told him yes and he proceeded to drive towards the arena. He continued to keep the conversation going with flattery and jokes. Money was kind of a good guy.

When we pulled up to the arena, Money climbed out and took my hand as we entered the building. He was smiling from ear to ear. He enjoyed having me as his trophy for the evening. He shook hands with other fans of the team and even slapped hands with a few of the players. Money made sure that I knew he was somebody in these Cleveland streets. He ordered us some drinks, we sat back, and enjoyed the game.

After the game, I was feeling a little tipsy. I couldn't believe how low my tolerance level was to liquor since I haven't really drunk in a while. Money and I must have had three glasses of wine before he started drinking beers like a sailor. He was happy because he claimed that he bet twenty thousand on the game and I was his good luck charm. I had to admit seeing his excitement made me feel good.

Before we had gotten far away from the arena, Money said that he had to make a quick stop. I could tell from his tone of voice that it was serious. I shook my head, set back, and rode. He got on his cell phone and started chewing somebody's ass out. He was talking to them like they were dumb asses.

Money drove down Superior heading for the east side of town. I recognized that the city was getting darker and darker. The street lights were even a dim yellow color, barely shinning any light on the neighborhoods. I knew that we were far away from the bright lights and busy streets of the downtown night life.

He pulled up in front of a chicken shack. The aroma from the chicken smelled delicious. I noticed customers standing inside waiting for their orders. From the looks of the line, I knew that the food was good as well. Some broasted wings sure did sound good right now.

"My mans inside. I have a little business to handle. You will be alright right here. Nobody will fuck with you. Trust me," he said opening the door.

"I'm not going to stay out here in this fucking car; waiting to get raped or something!" I said, sounding like a stuck up bitch.

Money chuckled.

"Trust me, you will be better in here than in there with some goons."

"I'll take my chances!" I snapped climbing out of the car.

Money continued to laugh believing that I was going to be scared of these crooks. Little did he know, I was born into this crime life. My brother and all of his friends were locked up for being drug traffickers.

We entered the chicken shack from the back. The door was cracked opened using a milk crate. He opened the door allowing me to enter first. I did notice a pistol on his hip. I didn't know if he was going to hurt somebody or he just had the gun for protection.

Money slapped hands with a big bald head brutha and whispered something that I couldn't hear. The man left the room in a hurry. I wondered what was the whispering for. I started to lean against the wall but I noticed dirty hand prints and I wasn't about to get my clothes filthy.

"Who's this bitch?" A younger man said staring me down.

Money didn't say a word as he rushed over to him. Money grabbed the man by his throat lifting him off of his feet. With his free hand he pulled out his gun and placed the barrel of the gun forcefully against the man's chest.

"Now apologize to my lady, before I empty this clip in your bitch ass!"

"I'm sorry man! I didn't know!" He screamed.

"No, apologize to her!" Money ordered.

"I'm sorry miss. I didn't mean to disrespect you."

"That's more like it," Money uttered.

Money smiled at me and walked over to the bald black man. The man had a clear plastic chicken shack bag full of money. My eyes widened at the bundles of cash in the bag. I was thinking about getting them then. They were just so freely open with conducting business in front of a total stranger. Money again whispered in his ear and signaled for us to leave.

I wanted to be nosy and all up in his business but I chose otherwise. I sat back listening to the music and allowed my mind to wonder. I figured that Money had loot all over the city. I had to act fast and I had three days to do it.

Money pulled up in front of the hotel and took a deep breath before he had spoken. He turned the music down low and stared at me. I felt him undress me with his eyes. I sat up to reach for my purse between my legs and he sneaked in a kiss on my cheek. I smiled and opened my door.

"Thanks for the good night but I must go to bed now. I have to meet my friends for breakfast in the morning," I said stepping out from the car.

At the last moment, Money asked to follow me up to my room. I know that he was going to try to make a move but I wasn't going to fall for it. I didn't want him to feel like I wasn't feeling him so I agreed and played along with his little game.

Now, as soon as I entered the hotel room he was right behind me. He brushed his dick against my ass stepping closer to me. I felt the bulge pressed against me and it felt like he was packing. I quickly walked in, placed my purse on the desk, and took a seat on the bed. I went to unzip the zipper on my heels. He rushed over; dropping to his knees and taking each shoe off. He placed my left foot against his broad chest and took my right foot in his hands. He began to rub my feet firmly, taking away the pain of wearing six inch heels all damn day. He then took each one of my toes into his mouth looking up at me seductively. I refused to entertain any of this smooth bullshit. I was aware of his tactics. I was going to keep my legs closed and mind focused.

Money finished sucking on my toes and began rubbing his hands up my legs towards my thighs, I quickly crossed my legs avoiding any touch on my goodies. His touch was soft but yet masculine. He asked me with his eyes to uncross my legs but I kept them tightly closed. I playfully pushed him away from the bed. He thought that I was serious and he inched towards the door.

"Money, I have something to keep me on your mind." I said seductively.

Money didn't seem upset about his failed attempt to get in my panties so I decided to give him a treat. A treat that would keep him wanting more. I lifted my legs and pulled off jeans revealing my caramel thighs. I kicked them off and waited to see his facial expressions. I spread my legs open wide and allowed him to have a direct look at my panties. He took a step closer but I waved for him to stop, which he did. I rubbed on my pussy slowly getting myself aroused. I felt myself becoming wetter. The wetness was soaking through my lace panties. I placed myself against the soft pillows sitting up, skillfully pulled my panties off, and threw them over to him. He kept his eyes on me as he bent over to pick my panties up from the floor. Money placed the panties against his nose taking a smell of my sweet scent. Pleased with the scent, he thanked me with a smile. I continued to give the man a show. I took my fingers and rolled them over my clit rapidly as if he wasn't in the room. I would switch my focus from my clit to diving my fingers inside of me. He was watching like a deer caught in head lights. His facial expression said it all. I knew that he was enjoying this show I was putting on. Thrusting my fingers inside of me I was able to make myself have a huge orgasm. I screamed filling the bedsheets with the squirt of my orgasm.

"Damn!" Money said excited. He licked his lips and walked over to the side of the bed.

"You want to taste this pussy?" I asked, pulling on his shirt.

"Hell yeah I do," he answered.

Money began grabbing his manhood like a little boy that had to pee badly. I couldn't help but find his thirst amusing. I took my fingers that remained to have my sweet nectar on it across his lips and into his mouth. He sucked on my fingers better than he was sucking on my toes earlier.

"Now if you like how my fingers taste wait until you taste the real thing," I teased.

"Why wait when I am here now?"

"Because, I am a lady and you have to earn this pussy."

"I respect that."

"I will see you tomorrow after I spend some time with my friends."

"Just give me a call and I will be by to pick you up," he said leaning in for a kiss.

I kissed him back so he wouldn't get any strange ideas.

Money left out of the room leaving me to feel disgusted.

Allowing another man touch on my skin had me feeling sick. I had to wash away the scent of the man, the touch, and thought of him.

I ended my night with a long hot shower. I gave myself some time to gather my thoughts. I tried to focus my attention on my next move with Money but Rashad seemed to appear out of the steam. He was like a ghost appearing right in front of me. I tried to catch my breath. Visions of my ex-husband ran through my mind. The thought of him beating me, cheating, kicking me out of our house, and fucking my best friend, and his death and me in shambles.

CHAPTER 3

The very next morning, I am awakened by the constant ringing of my cell phone. I hesitated to wake because of this headache. I believe the liquor got the best of me. Barely opening my eyes, the sun seemed to peek through the tan curtains and shine on me. I decided to get up and find out who's blowing me up this early in the morning. I was going to give them an ear full. I rolled over and closed the curtains before I even looked at my phone. I heard the phone ringing but didn't remember where I had placed it. The ringing sound was driving me insane. I flipped the sheets back and forth but came up empty. The ringing continued. I gave up and fell back on the pillows. Then I remembered that I had my phone in my pants when I took them off last night. I frantically crawl across the bed and grab my pants off the floor.

"Who is this?" I shouted into the phone.

"Tiana, it's me, Brian."

I hated when people called me my government name. My mother didn't even call me by my birth name. The streets called me Treasure because I was every man's dream. Nah, I'm just playing; that's just what I told myself. They called me Treasure because despite living in the hood and knowing that all of my friends lost their virginity by the age of fourteen, I was nineteen in college before I opened my legs. So everyone in the streets including my friends would say that I treated my pussy like it was treasure.

"Oh, I'm sorry baby. I had a rough night."

"A rough night?"

"Yeah, I stayed up drinking and watching Love and Hip Hop Atlanta on the DVR."

Brian laughed. "I don't see how you watch that shit."

"It's good baby. Maybe one day we will be on the show."

Brian laughed again. "Maybe so. Shit I will do it if the check is right."

"I know that's right."

Brian and I continued to talk as if I was at home waiting for his arrival. He didn't have any clue that I was out of town doing a job. And he wasn't going to find out. Brian knew about my past; but tried to make sure that I would never have to revisit that life. Honestly, I didn't have to but I was doing this for him.

After talking about daily shit, he asked what was I wearing. I knew that our conversation was going down another road. I played along with him. I didn't have any clothes on so I fed his imagination with some "white lies." Brian couldn't resist being away from home long and he confessed it was hard being away from this pussy. I had to keep him wanting more. Phone sex was the answer. I liked getting my man aroused just with words. Brian and I imagined making love to each other. I played with myself imagining his tongue swirling over my clit. He liked how I talked dirty to him. He begged for me to tell him what I would do if he was with me now. I said it directly as I imagined. He jerked off to my words causing himself to cum. I masturbated myself to have an orgasm too.

Shit- I did everything a wife was suppose to do according to my mother. My mother always told me to take care of my house, my man, and my family. I had to do what was needed from a wife at all times. If my job was to have phone sex with my husband, then so be it. If my job was to keep our love life spontaneous and maybe add a body, then so be it. I signed up for this job so I was going to do it. I wasn't going to lose another man because I wasn't taking care of home.

Brian wanted me to tell him what I had planned for his birthday but I wasn't going to give in. All he needed to know was that his birthday was going to be one that he would remember. The particulars wasn't needed. All he needed to know was that we were staying at the Palms hotel in Vegas and the flight we were taking.

After ending my conversation with Brian, I checked the time and decided to get my butt up. I had to do some more surveillance. I had planned on riding back past the chicken shack and Money's baby momma's house. These were two locations that he'd visited often so they were going to be the place where I planned on robbing him.

Within a matter of minutes, I was up and dressed. I pulled my hair back into a ponytail and threw on a jogging suit. I had a pair of fresh wheat Timb's that I couldn't wait to wear. Brian use to say that my Timb's matched my skin perfectly but I believed he said that so I wouldn't wear them. He would've rather saw me in a pair of heels to show off my legs any day. I reached into my suitcase and pulled out my new Glock 19. I put on some latex gloves and placed each bullet into the clip carefully. I was going to be prepared for anything including the opportunity to get Money when he had stacks of cash on him.

First, I made the drive past the chicken shack. I parked across the street at an old music store that was boarded up. People had cars for sell on the lot. I just parked in-between two of the cars and leaned back. I saw many customers go in and out but I didn't expect them of having anything in their bags besides food, until I saw the bald headed man. He pulled up and parked exactly were Money parked last night. He went in the same metal door carrying a duffle bag.

The sun began to set as the yellow lights flickered on. I cocked the gun back and waited to see the man or Money again. The nervousness that I had when I drove up disappeared. I was totally focused on my objective. I thought that maybe I could slide right out of the city after getting lucky with robbing the bald man. But with my luck I was going to handle this the good old fashion way and that was to use my ass to get what I wanted.

I sat in total darkness. The closes light-pole was about 25-30 yards away near a closed dollar store. The light was hesitating to fully turn on and buzzed like an annoying bumble bee. I was waiting on the perfect opportunity to present itself.

Suddenly, my other phone rang. The caller ID read, "Money." I hesitated to answer for a moment because I didn't want him asking me any questions about my whereabouts. Hopefully I wasn't caught sitting out here casing the joint. The light from my phone lit up the car so I answered and placed the phone to my ear.

"Hello," I said trying to sound normal.

"What's up sexy?" Money said smoothly.

"Nothing much. Getting ready to find me something to eat."

"Okay. Well I have a few things to handle but later I would like to see you."

"What is later?"

"Around ten. I have a place that I would like to take you."

"Ten? That's like two hours from now!" I snapped.

"What's wrong? Is that a bad time?"

"You know that I have to fix my make-up and pick out something nice to wear for you." I said simply.

"Well, where we are going, you don't have to worry about that."

"Where is that?" I asked.

"It's a place that I like to go to take my mind away from this street shit. I know that you will like the place."

"It sounds nice."

"It is."

"I am excited."

"Treasure, how does it sound to be a part of my fantasies?"

"Umm, I'm unsure." I said not knowing where the conversation was leading.

"I just want you to know that I am extremely attracted to you. After I left your hotel room, you stayed on my mind."

"Aww, how sweet. You had me thinking that you wasn't into me." I toyed with his head.

"I don't know what will make you think that. But don't worry, I will show you better than I can tell you. I just hope that you are ready for what I have planned for you."

"Oh I will be ready." I teased.

"I'll hold you to it." He giggled.

"Okay, pick me up at ten. I will be waiting for you."

After I ended my call with Money, I sat wondering what this fantasy thing was. Whatever he had in mind, he was excited about it. I wasn't about to fuck him or suck him off. What could this fantasy be?

The bald headed guy finally came out of the chicken shack. He had a duffle bag with one hand and a bag with the chicken shack logo on it in the other hand. I assumed that the money was in the chicken bag because that's how Money took his out of there the other day. I pulled on my door handle causing the dome light to turn on. I was out in the open for anyone to see. I managed to take a few steps away from the car before pulling out my piece. No one was on the block so I had to keep to the shadows and take my chance. He opened the trunk and was preparing to place the duffle bag inside but I darted across like a scared rabbit. My Timbs slapped against the pavement but didn't catch his attention. I didn't say a word as I pressed the barrel of the gun against his tailbone. He dropped the chicken bag onto the ground.

"Really. You really want to do this. You know that we are going to find out who you are and make your whole world crumble!" The bald man said.

Continuing to remain silent, he obeyed as if I was speaking. He took the bag out of the trunk and I spotted the shotgun laying near-by. I knew that I had to do something to keep him from being a hero. I snatched the duffle bag from his grasp and tried to figure out what to do next. He continued talking shit.

"Mutha fucka you are fucking with the wrong crew. We are going to get you back." He threatened.

I searched the streets looking for any witnesses. I knew that at any moment that someone was going to come out of the restaurant or pull up. I had to act fast. I quickly flipped the gun and was now holding the barrel in my hand. With the butt of the gun, I forcefully smacked him across the head. I thought that the force of the gun would knock him out but there he stood. Blood trickled from his head down to his lime green Polo shirt. Not knowing what else to do, I went on a rampage. I rapidly hit the man until he folded over and eventually hit the ground. I grabbed both of the bags and took off down the street on foot. Not wanting to dart directly for my car, I thought that it was a good idea to go in a different direction and then circle back around. I ran so fast that I thought that I was going to run out of my boots.

    I waited a few minutes outside of a dollar store watching the scene. I squatted next to a Red Box and tried to control my breathing. I took three deep breaths and smelled a familiar scent. I looked around for anyone that could have crept up on me but not a soul was in sight. I looked down at the bags and simultaneously searched the bags while I kept my eyes on the bald man. My nose finally found the scent that had my mind racing; inside of the chicken shack bag I found a box full of chicken wings and buttered wedges. I was pissed. I only hoped that the other bag didn't fool me. Soon as I stuffed my hands inside of the bag I felt something. I pulled out the items I recovered and to my surprise the bag was filled not with cash but five bricks of coke. The price for coke was high but the heroin would have been better to move. I believed that Money sold the heroin and his partner must have sold the dope. I wanted the money more than the dope but this was a start. I didn't sell dope but my brother and his friends had folks still on the streets that I could whole sell the shit to.

    Buzz, buzz… my cell phone vibrated in my pocket. I knew that the caller had to either be my mother about Raymond or Brian calling to get some more. Either way they had to wait until I was back in the hotel room. I didn't even bother taking out my phone to answer.

Finally, the young man whom called me a bitch the other day comes out. He took notice to his buddy knocked unconscious on the ground. He shook him and smacked him a few times getting the bald man to come to life. I could hear him from across the street yelling at the bald man asking "who did it." The young man helped the bald guy to his feet then set him in the back seat. They took off in the car racing down the street. I assumed he was rushing him to the near-by hospital.

I walked to my car like I was just taking a stroll in the neighborhood. I climbed into the car, threw the duffle bag on the passenger seat and drove off.

During the drive, I still felt unsatisfied. I contemplated on just leaving with the drugs but I knew that Money had plenty of cash around the city. I wasn't satisfied with this shit. At most I might get ten thousand a brick on the street knowing that it was hot. I wasn't working this hard for pennies.

When I arrived at my hotel, I received a text from Money saying that he might not be able to make our date. I acted foolish and asked why knowingly. He explained that his boy was in the hospital and he had to go see him. He said that he was unsure if he could see me after he left the hospital. I had to act fast. So I did what any other woman in my shoes would do, I assume. I sent him a picture of me looking sad without my bra on. He instantly took the bait. He texted that he would be on time.

Quickly, I climbed into the shower and washed my body. I went over my pubic hair making sure that it was neatly shaven just in case I was forced to do the imaginable for this money. I finished shaving my whole body until I was nice and smooth.

I lotion my caramel legs giving them the perfect shine. I sprayed perfume between my cleavage and wrist before putting on my dress. Although Money said that I didn't have to dress too fancy for wherever we were going, I had to keep his eyes glued on me. Tonight was going to be the night that I was going to get him for whatever he had to offer.

CHAPTER 4

Ring, Ring, Ring… I answered on the third seeing that it was Money. I had to make him wait for a minute. I didn't want him to think that I was too geeked up about our date.

"Hey sexy, I'm outside."

"Oh, okay. Give me a second."

"Do you need me to come up?"

"No. I'll be right down."

I hung up but I was feeling a little nervous. Why am I feeling like this? I wondered.

Without any time to waste, I rushed to the elevator and hurried to his car. Money opened the door for me again just like a gentleman. But when I went to sit I noticed a large shopping bag on the seat. I could recognize a Victoria Secret bag from miles away. I managed to peek inside of the bag and I see lingerie. I lifted the bag and placed it on my lap. Money closed my door and skipped over to his. Before I could thank him he reached behind my seat to get something. His chest was all in my face. I smelled the fresh scent of his cologne. It was so delightful. I closed my eyes and allowed the scent to take over me. The scent alone made me horny. I heard a plastic crumbling noise. I opened my eyes. Money had a bouquet of flowers in his hand.

"Thanks, the flowers are beautiful. I can't remember the last time I had a bouquet of flowers," I lied.

"Seriously?" Money asked.

"Seriously." I answered.

"If I was your husband, I would send you flowers every day. That mutha fucka doesn't know the beautiful flower that he has," Money said gripping the wheel.

I sat silent not objecting or agreeing with his statement. I didn't want to open any doors that didn't need to be opened. My silence must have given him the invitation to get a little closer. Money shifted himself into a relaxed position, then placed his right hand upon my thigh. I didn't move or give him any signs that I didn't want him to touch me. I relaxed and enjoyed the music as he drove us back near downtown.

We pulled up in front of a brick red building. The red brick was tattooed with graffiti. The building was surrounded by a tall black fence. A security guard stood at the fence and allowed us to enter. Money parked the car next to a Bentley coupe. He looked at me waiting for me to say something. I was lost for words. I mean I didn't have a clue where he was taking me. This building looked more ran down than the chicken shack he had taken me to. The building looked like an abandoned manufacturing building that had been out of business for decades.

"It's cool. Trust me." Money smiled.

"Are you sure?" I questioned looking at him funny.

"Yes. It gets better inside." He continued to smile.

"Well if you say it's cool."

"It's cool."

Money came around the car and opened my door. "Don't forget to bring your bag," Money said pointing at the bag of lingerie. He helped me walk on the gravel parking-lot because if not I would have fell smack on my face. He laughed as I danced on the rocks headed for the door. I felt a sense of relief when I saw smooth asphalt near the door.

Money rang the doorbell and another security guard opened the door momentarily. The security guard was this cute white man. He looked ex-military with his physique and buzz haircut. His ripped chest stood out from his tight V-neck T-shirt that read "security" in big white letters. He shook Money's hand firmly and allowed us to enter. I noticed him continuing to check me out as we walked away.

Soon as we entered we were greeted by a beautiful waitress. She was topless and although her breasts were clearly fake, they sure did look great. Her skin was beautiful and her smile was inviting. Money leaned down and gave her a kiss on the cheek. I could tell that they were very familiar with each other. She looked me up and down and smiled like I was a piece of meat. Money ordered us some drinks and slapped her on the ass as she turned away.

Money turned to talk to the security guard and I stood wondering where he had brought me. I wondered was this a private party? Was this a low key tittie bar? I stepped away from Money trying to figure things out. I looked down the corridor and I didn't see anything. All I could do was wonder. My ears suddenly caught a female's laughter.

Money walked up behind me and wrapped his muscular arms around my waist, "Are you ready to have some fun?"

"If you are." I answered frowning my face, but he couldn't see it.

We crept down the corridor and a totally naked woman almost scared me half to death standing in the doorway of a room. I jump back into Money's arms and he burst out laughing. The woman slowly closed the door allowing me to peek inside. I noticed one of the ball players from the other night laid back with his shirt off being fed some grapes from another totally naked woman. *What kind of place was this?*

Money and I continued to stroll down the corridor passing by multiple rooms. Every room there had a different sound coming from the door. I heard laughter, moans, screams, music, and straight out fucking noises. The lights down the corridor fucked with my eyes. The strobe light flickered like I was slowly walking through time. We reached the end of the corridor and Money pulled on my arm to go right. I looked behind us and noticed more women prancing around in different costumes. My mind was dancing with so many weird images that I saw before me.

Money took out his keys and opened the first door that we came upon. I wondered, *'was this nigga a V.I.P. member for this spot?'*

When he opened the door; there were two people monitoring the cameras throughout the place, another counting money, and an old black lady shuffling through cards that read "Fantasy Island." The money was being tossed into red plastic tubs. Money went over to the person handling the money and I turned my attention to the cameras. I mean there must have been over twenty rooms with different themes in them. I saw threesomes, men on men, men dressed like babies, women being gang fucked by three or four men, little people having sex, girls on girls, whatever you could imagine was in front of me. I went into a trace like state looking at all of this madness.

"All right momma, keep up the good work." Money said kissing the old black woman.

Does this fool really have his mother working in here? Weirdo!

"Money, what the fuck is this shit?" I asked sounding pissed off.

"This is one of my most profitable businesses."

"You mean, you own this?" I asked pointing at the cameras.

"Hell yeah I do! This club alone makes me a little over a million dollars a year."

"Really?" I said amazed.

"Look at this scene here. This man is a congressman's assistant and he's a loyal customer. He spends about five stacks a month. Oh, and look here. This guy here plays ball for Cleveland and he is in here after every home game. And he spends about ten thousand a week during the season."

"Damn! You are really getting paid then!"

"Exactly! There's nothing wrong with fulfilling someone's most desired fantasies now is it?"

"Um, no I guess." I said, trying to give it some thought.

"Come on with me."

Money and I walked to an entirely different part of the building. I knew that it was more discreet because the sounds from the other rooms faded away. The waitress was right behind us with bottles and rushed ahead into the room.

Two Latin looking woman were already sitting on the edge of the bed when we entered through the purple and red curtains; which covered the door. Incense filled the air, giving the room an inviting fragrance. The lights throughout the room were tainted blue; not too dark that I couldn't look around. I inched closer to the women because I was curious to what they were wearing. In the far back of the room, I noticed a rack full of bondage sex toys. I mean there were paddles, whips, feathers, handcuffs, and restraints. I knew exactly what this room was for.

One of the women only had on a pair of crotchless beaded thong panties with a bow in the back. Her pussy was shaven and clean. It looked as if she had just got it waxed. She wore chained nipple clamps which kept her nipples erect with every move she made. The other woman had on a sexy body stocking outfit revealing her bare ass.

The curvy one with the crotchless panties went over to the corner and pulled out what I believed was a chair until I noticed handcuffs and ankle cuffs attached. It was a bench made for restraining your subject and making them suffer with pleasure or pain. She bent over and started cuffing her ankles giving Money and I a direct view of her pussy. The other girl walked over to assist her. I knew that something was about to go down. I stepped closer for more of a better viewing.

In the far back of the room, I noticed a rack full of bondage sex toys. I mean there were; paddles, whips, feathers, handcuffs, and restraints. I am curious to know how most of these items work. I knew exactly what this room was for. But I didn't know why he chose me to come in here.

Money nudges me, "You can join in if you like."

"Who me?" I asked knowingly.

"Why not you?"

"Be... Because." I stuttered.

"You said that you were willing to be a part of my fantasies, well this is it. I told you that I would hold you to it."

"Well, I guess I can."

"Bet. You can change right over there." Money said pointing at another room.

Inside of the private room, I changed into the lingerie that Money bought for me. Surprisingly the clothes fit me precisely. The thong hugged my hips showing nothing but ass and my fat ass pussy lips. I couldn't hide my lips even if I wore granny panties. My pussy just poked out. The bra was actually cute also. It was lavender with a small pink bow in-between my breasts. The peek-a-boo cutouts were perfect for this setting. The bra shaping my breasts allowed them to sit up like I was wearing a push-up bra.

I talked myself into going through with this fantasy of his no matter what. My eyes began to fill with tears just thinking about going through with it. I managed to get myself together before a tear ran down my face. I took out my body spray and sprayed my breasts and over my pussy again just to strengthen my scent. I had hide my Glock under my clothes and placed it back in the bag neatly folded. I wasn't going to leave it in my purse for one of the bitches to be nosy.

When I came out, the girls were making out. They were feeling on each other and kissing like they were really enjoying it. Money just watched and played with himself. The curvy girl was in a good position for anything. I had to admit that this was different. I grabbed the paddle and begun to spank her.

"Okay Treasure! I see you!" Money cheered.

"You like that?" I teased.

"Yeah but do it harder!" Money shouted.

Bam! Bam! Bam!

The girl screamed sensually, "Oh!"

I was actually enjoying it. Money was also. Before I knew it, Money was out of his clothes and laid back on the bed watching us put on a show.

Money put the slightly thinner girl onto a door swing. She sat on the swing awaiting for him to come inside of her. The swing had a padded cradle for Money to sit on with adjustments for different positions. Money grabbed leverage on two handles above him and in an athletic position slid his dick right into her.

While Money was fucking her, I continued to pleasure the other girl. She asked to switch but I played it off and told her that she was a bad girl. I spanked her until I saw Money from the corner of my eye adjusting himself in the swing.

Money climbed out of the sling and proceeded to eat the girl out. I watched him as he danced his tongue on her pussy. I had to admit that Money had a nice looking ass for a man. It was muscular like the rest of his body. I stood and studied his muscular body. He had a tattoo of the city of Cleveland skyline on his back along with the logos of the pro teams from the city. He had another tattoo of his son's face on his ribs. The tattoo that had me interested was one that was across his right shoulder blade. The name read 'Shaniqua.' Who the fuck was Shaniqua? I know that couldn't be his mother's name.

After a few more spanks, I untie the girl. She got up and gave me a kiss gripping my ass. I didn't resist her touch and I actually played along. I grabbed her ass and we shared a passionate kiss. When we separated I told her to bring Money over to the bed. I watched her ass jiggle as she walked over to Money. She did what I had instructed and got his full attention. Money untied the young lady and helped her to get out of the swing. I stood there patiently waiting. When I caught Money's eye, I knew that I had to do something to keep his attention. *'If this fool had everything that a man could want sexually, what could I do?'*

I waited until Money was in arms reach of me and then I turned for the bed. I put on the best runway strut a woman could walk. The girl didn't have nothing on me. I studied the model Deelishis like I wanted to be her. I shifted my hips with control working my ass for his eyes and for whoever else who was watching. I looked over my shoulder and like I figured, his eyes were glued on my ass along with the two girls. I bet he imagined how my ass would look in these thongs he had bought for me.

I stopped in front of the bed and turned to him. Without any touch from me I noticed his manhood growing. I forcefully grabbed it knowing that he was into that rough shit. He frowned at first then quickly changed his facial expression to joy. I tugged on his penis getting him fully hard while the girls were placing kisses on his lips and chest. I turned him around and pushed him down to the bed. The ladies assisted me with tying his wrist and ankles onto the bed.

I pulled off my panties, and then he yelled "Oh shit!" I threw my panties at him. He started squirming in the bed ready to get a piece of my cookie. Both of the girls shared his dick with their tongue. I stood watching while I pulled off my bra and tossed it to the floor. I covered my body with baby oil to give it a nice shine. Although the girls were sucking him off he kept his eyes on me. I started to dance to the music imagining I was stripping again. I twerked my ass like I was getting paid for it. I bounced my ass to the rhythm of the rap music that was being softly played through the speakers. I took everyone's attention and now the girls were even taking notes. I bent over continuing to twerk and slid my middle finger between my pussy lips slowly. I was so wet that I heard my pussy moaning. I put my finger inside my mouth and teased him with the thought of tasting me. I stood straight up and turned to them. The thick girl rushed to grab a condom from her bag. She slid the condom down to the base of his dick and then climbed on. I knew that she was trying to steal back his attention but I wasn't in competition with her, I was here to do a job. I giggled at her actions. I went to the side of the bed and climbed on his face for him to taste my sweat nectar.

I sat on his face and bounced my ass off of his chin. The tip of his tongue was pressed against the tip of my clit. I reached down and grabbed his head with my hands, "Lick that pussy baby." I worked my pussy harder against his tongue. He rolled his tongue harder and faster getting every last drop. Money slapped me on the ass getting me more excited. Before I knew it, my legs began to shake and I let go.

I stood up and looked at him giving him my gratitude. I couldn't lie, the man did his damn thang on the pussy. He sure did know how to eat some pussy. I didn't think that I was going to enjoy it as much as I did. But I am thankful that I gave myself the needed pep talk.

The girls continued to fuck him until he came. Luckily we wore his ass out! After the girls put it on him, all he wanted to do was drink and talk about sex some more. He insisted that we all get together again. I was the first to say that I was down for it. I put my official stamp on it when the girls and I made out for his pleasure.

CHAPTER 5

Today was the last day of for my plan to manifest. It was either now or never. And I didn't put in all of this work for a good head job and a few bricks of coke. I had to get my hands on the loot. I had a few options in mind, but I had to first see if I could work my hand with his baby momma.

I didn't know if they were really close but from her actions, I knew that they weren't in a relationship. Shit, she didn't even allow the fool inside of her home. To me, it looked like they were just playing their positions of being parents.

The temperature outside was perfect. High in the mid 80's and a lot of sun shine. I pulled out a pair of tight jean shorts and a white tank top to show off my breasts. The six inch heels added another sexy dimension to my legs. I was going to match this woman's beauty. I stood in the mirror for over an hour curling my hair and making sure that it was on point like I had just left the shop. Before I walked out of the hotel room, I made sure that my gun was in my purse and my lip gloss was on point.

After I checked out of the hotel and allowed the hotel staff to put my bags into the trunk of my car, I drove off. The time was nearing when she would take their son to the daycare and I wanted to follow her everywhere she went.

My plan was for the girl and I to get friendly and then I was going to snatch her ass up and take her for a ride back down to the city. Money was going to have to pay me for getting a chance to taste my goodies and to get the mother of his child back. I wanted a hundred large; period point blank. I wasn't going to accept nothing less. I knew he had it; from the buckets of cash at the weird night club and the shit I heard on the streets. A hundred stacks wouldn't even dent his pockets.

    I parked three houses down from her house and just like clockwork, she pulled out in her A6 Audi and drove off. The woman had good taste in cars because we had the same car but different colors. I stood two to four cars away from her the whole time. The daycare was only about an eight-minute drive from her home. I watched her take her son into the building and minutes later, rush back out. I followed her to the grocery store and I waited outside. She came out about ten minutes later with a bottle of wine and a single bag of groceries.

    She sped off back to her house. She was driving like she knew I was behind her or she had somewhere to be. I mean, she was zooming through yellow lights and barely stopping at stop signs. The only reason why I was able to stay close to her was because I knew where she was going. We were in her neighborhood so I knew she was rushing to get back home. I was going to take the first opportunity I had to get her when she would least expect it.

    When I finally arrived on her block, she was pulling her car into the garage. I rushed to put the car in park and took out my pistol from my purse. I quickly climbed out, looking around for nosy neighbors. I mean, it seemed like nobody had to work today. Neighbors were out washing their cars, mowing grass and planting. I noticed her next door neighbors, an old couple, chilling on their porch sharing a conversation. I decided to go against my plan and wait for another chance. I was going to camp out in my car, but I could bring attention to myself.

I jumped back in the car and circled the block finding a perfect camp spot under an old walnut tree. The shade hid my face and I had a clear view of her front door.

Suddenly, as I pushed the door of my car open, a marron Ford F-150 with an American flag on the back pulled up in her driveway in a hurry. I gently closed my door and watched closely. I couldn't see who it was, but I assumed it was a male because of the large cowboy hat. I didn't see his face until he waited at the door for her to answer. The man looked all too familiar. Within a second, I figured where I knew the man's face from. He was from Money's nasty night club. He was the fine ass white security guard that was working inside last night. *'What was he doing here?'*

I went ahead and climbed out. I looked in both directions for any witnesses and the old couple remained sitting on their porch. I had to go about this differently. I thought of maybe just simply knocking on the door and asking about Money. I also thought about pretending to be a saleswoman for an energy company or cable network hoping that she would allow me in without any struggle. It would be a shame if I had to mess her pretty little face up.

Walking up the driveway, I waved 'hi' to the old couple on the porch. They waved back with a friendly smile. I didn't want to alarm them with any suspicion. I took a look inside of the truck and noticed two Monster energy drinks. I assumed he was getting ready to burn off a lot of calories with what he had in mind. With soft knocks I knocked on the door. I waited gripping my gun. Nobody answered. I walked to the side of the house looking for an opening and I stumbled up on a cracked window near the backyard. I braced myself against the stone wall of the house and listened. I can hear her moaning and him also making noises. They didn't waste any time. The window was only about a few inches above my head. So grabbed hold onto a stone pulling myself up. I stood on the tips of my toes and peeked in. Luckily I had these heels on to add a few inches to my size.

Money's baby momma was totally naked laid out on the granite kitchen island. The man was standing next to her wearing only his cowboy boots and hat. I had an easy view of his penis and I was not impressed at all. He might have been 4 and a half maybe five inches at best. His penis was fat though so I guess she enjoyed that part of the deal. '*I guess you can't always have it all.*'

I watched the man feed her chocolate covered strawberries. Then he reached inside of the cabinet and took out a bottle of Hersey chocolate syrup; the kind of syrup you put on vanilla ice cream. But this man decides to circle it over her nipples. He dove in, sucking the chocolate off of each nipple. She sat up and gave him a kiss. I noticed that while she was kissing him her legs slowly parted further apart. I wasn't the only one who took notice either. The man placed his right hand upon her toned stomach and begun to travel his hand between her thighs. I watched him slide his fingers inside of her. After a few moments of finger fucking her, he took the chocolate syrup and drew a line from the bottom of her lip to the tip of her clit. He started to scroll his tongue from her lip down her neck and I thought that now was the time to get my ass in there somehow.

I ran to the back of the house and noticed white French doors. I tried to gently turn the knob but it was locked. I looked for anything in the yard that I could use to sneak in the kitchen window but not a board, toy, or brick was in sight. I crept back to the front of the house and to my surprise the old couple had left from their porch. I felt a sense of relief. I dug in my pockets and pulled out my latex gloves. While I was putting the last glove on, I noticed from the corner of my eye a patrol car. I quickly ducked in front of the truck. I was beginning sweat from the heat of the engine and afternoon sun. The patrol car slowly crept down the block and didn't seem to pay me any mind. I finally came out and the patrol car was about two blocks down the street.

'Close call.'

I went back to the front door, tried to turn the knob and like magic it opened. My heart skipped a beat thinking of someone being on the other side of the door. I poked the barrel of the gun inside the crack as I skillfully stepped in without making a sound. I turned back to quietly close the door. I noticed that she had tile floors in her foyer and I didn't want to get caught making a sound. So I squatted down and took off my heels and placed them near the door like I was an invited guest. I tip toed through the foyer with my aim pointed for whatever that was ahead of me. You would have thought that I was trained by the Columbus Police Force the way I held my gun and crept through her place.

I reached the formal sitting room and saw nice pieces of furniture and artwork. I would've loved to have this art in my place. The sex sounds became more clear. Both of them were moaning and talking shit to one another. I continued to inch down the hall until my eyes seen what my ears had already known. The man was in a chair facing me and she was bouncing up and down on his lap. From my view I could clearly see his dick going in and out of her. Money's baby momma was going wild. Looked like she was pretending to ride a wild horse the way she was hopping all over the man's lap. Shit! She basically was because I didn't see a condom on the man's penis. She even had his cowboy hat on and was holding on to the hat with one hand and was choking him with the other. The man had to be enjoying it. His face was flushed red and his eyes was tightly closed.

"Shaniqua that pussy is so good." The man said.

"Shaniqua." I whispered. Then it came to me. The tattoo on Money's shoulder was his baby momma's name. That nigga was in love for real and she's in here going hard on this other mutha fucka's dick.

She began to work her ass in some sort of way that I had never seen before. It was like she was trying to pop a joint or something. He was loving it, forcing her back down when she would pop.

She kind of reminded me of the shy stripper in the club that was trying to twerk like a sistah. It was killing me to watch this shit. This girl needed to attend some of my Anna's pole dancing classes. Nothing about her moves were sexy to me or arousing. I couldn't help but laugh at their actions alarming them.

"AW!" She screamed.

"Bitch calm the fuck down! You wasn't doing that much screaming just a second ago." I ordered pointing my gun directly at him.

"What!" He shouted, looking around her large breast.

"No, don't stop for me. Continue. You need a lot of work sistah."

The man began to move, "Hold on now G.I. Joe. You don't want to be laid up at the national cemetery. Now do you?"

He quickly sat back down. His little dick fell down a couple more inches almost disappearing in his pubic hairs.

"Get your ass up!" I ordered her.

She climbed off slowly and stared at me, "What are you here for?"

"Your baby daddy sent me."

"Walter sent you to kill me?" Shaniqua asked, starting to cry.

"Walter?"

"Money!"

"I know you from somewhere." The man interjected.

"No mutha fucka. You don't know me!"

"You was with him last night. Yes, I remember you." He said looking at me.

"Are you another one of his crazy girlfriends? I don't know why his bitches always want to attack me. I am not with him! Fuck!" She said sounding like a proper white girl. If I would've closed my eyes, I would have sworn that she was white.

"No. I'm not one of his crazy ass bitches. I barely even know Money. This is about the hundred thousand he's going to have to pay me or he will be attending your funeral."

"No! No! No! You can't kill me."

"I don't want to but if he don't give up the money, then I have to do what I have to do."

"I... I have a son." She stuttered crying.

As a mother I felt her pain. Having to raise my son alone was hard. I had to play both of the parental roles in his life. I couldn't leave her son to be raised by that weird mutha fucka. He would just raise his son to be another weird mutha fucka like him and his mother.

"Bitch, I know that y'all have a son! He goes to Babies and Tots Daycare. Matter of fact you should be going to pick him up around 4 o'clock correct?"

"Yes," she cried shivering.

"We might be able to work out something." I uttered, not believing that I managed to spit those words from my mouth.

"What? Anything," She said jumping up and down causing her breasts to bounce.

The man grabbed her hand for a sense of relief.

"I need a hundred thousand."

"I don't have it." She cried.

"That mutha fuckin' baby daddy of yours has it!"

"I know he does. That's why I am about to lose my child to him."

The man stood up and held her as she cried in his arms. I mean the woman was sobbing. He continued to stare at me with hopes that I didn't pull the trigger.

"Put y'all clothes on!" I ordered pointing with my gun at the pile of clothes on the floor.

We sat down and she told me about the hard divorce that Money was taking her through. He wanted custody of their child and he wanted the car he had bought her for an anniversary gift. He was so petty that he wanted the wedding ring, too. He threatened to

THE STREETS CALL ME TREASURE 2

have her put out on the street if she didn't sign the proper paperwork giving him custody. Money said that he would give her the weekend to have their son so he could run the streets. Her words were making me upset with the thought of the man he was. She couldn't afford a good lawyer to represent her because she was working at a hotel as a hostess. She barely made enough to put food on the table, but this nigga had courtside seats at the Cavs games. Not to mention the tubs of cash at the freaky deaky nightclub. I had to help her.

The two of them were barely dressed as Shaniqua and I continued to talk. Zack had on a tank top and a pair of boxer briefs. I thought men wore them to show off their goods but Zack didn't have much to show. She sat on Zack's lap wearing only a black silk flower-printed robe. Shaniqua would often open her legs to cross them and I would catch her showing me a little too much. I wasn't even looking hard either. It was right there. She would lift her legs high before shifting to the other leg. *'I had the mind to think that she was trying to test me.'* The more that she continued to talk, the more I realized what we had in common. I was not surprised to hear that she was a former Miss Michigan. Money met her at a party near her hometown of Flint.

All three of us had our own reasons to get Money. Zack wanted to be with Shaniqua for obvious reasons. I could look in his eyes and read how he felt about Shaniqua. He came up with the perfect plan. Instead of me getting Money for whatever he would give for his child's mother, I could get guaranteed money. His plan was for him to get me back inside without Money's escort. When I would enter he would sneak me the key to the security room where he keeps the money. Shaniqua and I agreed for her to get the security footage and have her weak ass lawyer use the footage as leverage in their case. I tossed around the idea in my head, but I wasn't for sure if I was going to give her the footage. While she was talking about the footage, I ignored her and zoned out thinking of other ways to use the footage for my benefit; not hers. When I came back to reality, I told her that I would make sure that she would at least have the money to get away and have the lawyer's money ready to go to bat. I agreed to give her a quarter of whatever I took. The only problem was keeping Money away from the club.

  Zack and I went through many different ideas on how to keep Money out of the club, but we would always drop the idea. We didn't have a for sure way to keep him from coming to the club and noticing me there. He would definitely know that something was up if I had showed up without his hand. Shaniqua cleared her throat and came up with a fantastic idea. Shaniqua would get Money over her house and do whatever it took to keep him there. We both knew that Money would jump at any opportunity to get something that he really couldn't get. Having a chance to fuck his baby momma again was well worth not being in the streets or at the nightclub. And if I didn't know better, she was eager to fuck him. The dick she'd been getting lately was whack and a woman only could take so much.

  Shaniqua got on the phone and called the daycare and requested that they keep her son a while longer. Then she added that she would have her cousin come by to pick him up when she had gotten off of work. The daycare must have been familiar with her cousin because Shaniqua didn't have to put up with a debate or argument with them. They agreed with her plans and Shaniqua ended her call.

  Zack finished getting fully dressed and looked at his watch checking the time. He claimed that he had to check in for work by 6 o'clock. It was time to get the plan in full swing. I watched

Shaniqua walk Zack to the door. Zack gave her a long kiss and skipped out of the door all happily. She turned around smiling. I couldn't figure this bitch out for nothing. I looked out the window and watched Zack pull out the driveway and zoom up the street. I managed to remember his license plate before he got away.

"Treasure, you can take a shower down here and I will take one in the master." Shaniqua said pointing in the direction of a guest room near the living room.

"Okay thank you."

"Do you think this plan will work?" She asked.

"Girl - one thing that I know about a man, is that you can hurt him through his pants or his pockets. We are getting both."

"I hope so. I can't let him have my son."

"He won't get him, but you need to do whatever you have in mind to keep him out the way."

"I will."

"Are you okay?"

"Yes. It's just that, I honestly still love him but…"

I cut her off, "Girl, you don't have to say another word. Trust and believe that I understand. I had to fight that demon before. But, Money is a dog. All he wants to do is hurt you. If he truly loved you, he would let you be and find love again."

"I hear you."

"Girl, if you only knew what that man does over at that club of his," I added.

"I do know. That's why I left his ass. He couldn't keep his thang in his pants."

"He's a dog!"

"I allowed him to fuck them girls and he just continued after I told him to stop."

"Shaniqua, you should take this money and get the fuck out of Cleveland. Take your son to Orlando. I know he wants to see his favorite Disney characters."

"Yeah, that will be nice." She laughed.

"Well, just do what's best for you and your son."

"I will."

After bringing my bags into the house, I found the room that she'd directed that I use to shower in. I closed the door behind me and took out my last dress that I hadn't yet worn. It was a bad ass dress that Brian bought me when he was down in Atlanta. The dress was a long, white, deep plunge neckline maxi dress with the splits on the side. I loved the dress because it showed off my breasts and my legs. I couldn't wait to put the dress on and felt the breeze of the wind blowing within it. The dress was pretty, but yet sexy. I decided against wearing any panties. I wanted to feel the cool night air.

I entered the bathroom and it was lovely. I had to admit that the girl could decorate. She had beautiful flowers in a pretty vase, scented candles to match the stone and towels, and more pictures. I took it upon myself to light three candles and place them around

THE STREETS CALL ME TREASURE 2

the garden tub. I felt right at home. The girl even had my favorite bath soap. I filled the tub with hot water along with some squirts of the white Dove body-wash. The scent from the candles and soap relaxed me. I dropped my clothes to the floor and slowly slid under the bubbles. I kept my gun in arms reach, but I didn't believe that I had to worry about Shaniqua trying anything stupid.

While I sat in the tub, my mind began to race with the thought of being set up. Zack could give me up to Money or even worse have me robbed when I stepped out of the club with the money. I need an incentive. I sat thinking what could I do. Then it dawned on me. I had to keep the club footage for myself. Giving her the footage was totally out of the question. I know that she wanted it badly for court to kill Money's character as a father, but fuck her feeling! I had to look out for me first. Worst case scenario; I would have to snatch up their little one and that was something that troubled me.

I must have been in the tub for over an hour. I didn't realize the bath water was becoming cold. I hopped out, ready to get dressed and realized that I didn't have a towel. I looked at her pretty decorative towels hanging on the stainless steel towel rack but I wasn't going to be disrespectful. I carefully opened the door not to allow the cool air to hit my body. I hated being cold.

Soon as I took a step out of the bathroom Shaniqua was waiting on me. She was lucky that I didn't have my finger on the trigger because she would have been blown away. But to my surprise she was bringing me a towel. She looked at my body dripping water onto her bamboo floors. I continued to walk directly for her.

"You have a beautiful body," Shaniqua said continuing to study my body.

"Thank you. You do too."

"Not like yours. Look at all of that ass on you girly." She laughed.

"It's not much, but thank you. I see you've gotten yourself ready for your baby daddy." I said looking at the lingerie she was wearing.

"I wanted to get your opinion on this little thing."

"It's remarkable."

"I planned on wearing it later but when he first comes in, I'm coming out of it."

"You might as well not wear anything at all. Surprise him at the door with your birthday suit."

"Damn girl. You are a real freak! It's an awesome idea and I am going to do it."

Shaniqua giggled with the thought as she walked out of the room.

I softly patted my skin with the towel that Shaniqua had for me. The air had my nipples hard. Since I was already in my birthday suit, I decided to apply lotion over my body. I sat on the side of the bed facing the door taking out the bottle of pearberry lotion from Bath and Body Works. I rubbed the lotion over my breasts down to my stomach. I could hear Shaniqua in the kitchen moving around, but I wasn't paying her any mind. I knew that she was prepping for Money's arrival. Not able to rub my whole body from a seated position, I stood up and placed my foot on the bed. I squirted the lotion in my hands and eased my hands down my legs. Again, I squirted a quarter size amount into my hands rubbing them together.

"You need some help?" Shaniqua asked.

I instantly dropped the lotion bottle on the floor. I looked up and Shaniqua was standing near the doorway.

"No I am fine." I answered with a gentle smile.

"You smell good. So good that I could taste it."

'Was this woman really trying to hit on me?'

Although she was a beautiful woman, I wasn't about to touch her. I was so focused on the object at hand. She had two wine glasses in her hand and started to walk towards me. I continued to lotion my ass and lower back while she studied my every move.

Ring! Ring!

"Oh shit that has to be Walter! I texted him; telling him to come over," Shaniqua said running off to the sound of her cell phone.

'Saved by the bell.'

I finished getting dressed and quickly put on some lip gloss with some eye shadow. I was a pro when it came to the make-up. It looked as if I had my eyes professionally done by a make-up artist. I added a little glitter on top of my cleavage to capture a few more eyes when I stepped into the building. I had to make sure that I was looking good and sexy.

I went back out to the living room and I overheard Shaniqua's and Money's conversation. She sounded just like me; trapping that fool with some good ass pussy. She was teasing him with ideas of her sucking his dick and riding it to his delight. I laughed hearing her talk to him. I knew his thirsty ass would be over here in a heartbeat wanting to get some of that "baby momma pussy." I waved bye and headed for the door with my things.

    The sun was beginning to set as I walked out of Shaniqua's house. The sky was a lovely dark orange color; almost red. The street was quiet and still. The only person I could see was the old man now alone sitting on his porch. He kept his eyes on me as I walked to the back of my car. Although he didn't say a word, he was talking with his eyes. I bet he kept his eyes on Shaniqua's chocolate body everyday also. I placed my bags into the trunk and played with the man by blowing him a kiss. He grinned and stood up like he was about to run across the street. I laughed at the thought of him getting excited and climbed in the driver's seat. I started the car and turned the air on cool to keep my body from sweating. I hooked up my phone to my speakers and selected my music. I pulled off blasting the artist Stalley 'Jackin Chevys' to get my mind set for the heist.

CHAPTER 6

When I arrived at Money's nightclub, the same guard from the other night was at the parking-lot again. I prayed that he didn't recognize me being with Money last night. I rolled my window down and allowing him to walk up to the door.

"Hi cutie." I said smiling hard like I was taking pictures.

"Hello." The man said almost sticking his whole head inside of the window. His eyes were right where I wanted them; on my breasts. I didn't want him to recognize me, but he sure could get some eye candy.

"Is it a nice crowd in there? I am looking to have a little fun tonight." I said seductively.

"Yes, it's thick in there. I believe some rappers or ball players are coming tonight. So, the ladies are ready to get nasty if you know what I am talking about."

"I sure do."

"You can park right over there."

"Okay, well let me get in and enjoy myself."

I pulled off slowly. I made sure that I didn't kick up any gravel to hit the man or scratch up the paint on the car.

After parking the car, I placed my gun in my purse. I took a deep breath before I opened the door. I looked at myself in my rearview-mirror and coached myself to go through with it. I felt a little nervous. There wasn't going to be any turning around once I opened the door. I took one last deep breath and then opened the door; putting my heel into the gravel.

When I stepped out, the wind caught my dress revealing my bare ass and goodie box. The guard's eyes were on me and he smiled at the sight of my dress blowing in the air. I didn't even bother to try to hold the dress down and walked fiercely towards the door like a runway model.

As I walked, I searched the area for any sign of Money. I didn't see his car or his right hand man's car. A sense of relief came over me and my nervousness soon faded away. Before I rung the doorbell, I searched the lot again. I was looking for any sign of some ballers' whips. I noticed three or four fifty thousand dollar cars, but nothing to suspect that a rich mutha fucka was inside. The lot wasn't as full as last night but I still imagined that some weird mutha fucka was in here wasting their money on wild fantasies.

Again, I was happy to reach the paved area. I gently pushed on the doorbell and it buzzed annoyingly. The door slowly opened allowing the noise and club light to spill out. I hesitated to step in until I saw a friendly face; Zack. He patted me down gently. He seemed as if he was scared to touch me. He asked me to unzip my purse. I did what I was told. He didn't even look in the purse and like the other guard, he kept his eyes on my breasts. This man was infatuated with curvy black women. Smoothly, he dropped a key into my purse and then looked into my eyes. I knew that the key belonged to the security door that held the money and club footage.

"It's an alright crowd in here today but the high rollers are on their way. They gave us a call about twenty minutes ago. I think you should wait to make your move if you want the real money. I will give you the signal and then you just hit the room." Zack whispered in my ear.

I played along smiling like I was hearing the best lines from a man. Zack started to move his head away from my ear. I thought quickly and give him a kiss on the cheek. It was the same move that Money did on the waitress last night. This would make anyone who was watching believe that I was a regular or knew Zack well. He played along and placed his hands right above my ass and kissed me back. Although it was just a peck on my cheek, it was enough to make the scene look good.

Zack suddenly got on his walkie talkie, "Ronnie, I need you up front."

"I'm on my way." The man said on the other end.

Zack waited, not saying a word to me and looking down the corridor. I noticed the waitress from last night coming towards us. I tried to look back at the entrance door, but I didn't want to look foolish. I turned my head back towards her and looked directly into her eyes. Her face was fierce. She seemed as if she was mad about something.

"Zack, them fools are back in here!" She shouted over the noise of the club.

"The pimps?"

"Yes!"

"I didn't let them in!"

"Somebody did!"

"They're not VIP so they must have come through the front entrance. Ronnie must have let them in."

"Ronnie should know not to let them in. Didn't y'all take their membership cards?"

"I would have to ask Momma Kathy."

"Well them fools are being rude as usual! Grabbing me and the other waitresses. Not to mention that they are in here just to snatch one of these bitches up."

"I will handle it, but let me first escort our guest here to her room."

The waitress didn't even look my way and rolled her eyes walking away. I assumed she didn't expect to hear that Zack wasn't on it like she was. Zack waited to speak as he watched her get out of hearing distance.

"I'm going to hit the lights in the building causing chaos and you do whatever it is you do."

"Will there be any other guards in the room?"

"No."

"That's crazy!"

"Money doesn't think that anybody has the balls to try something like this."

"They don't! She has a pussy."

"I am going to take you to the party room. Just sit back and wait for my signal."

"Party room?"

"It's our best room for first time guest and people that like to have multiple partners."

"I'm not a first time guest."

"You're right, but you can blend in with the other guests in the party room."

The guard Zack was talking to, started to come towards us. We stopped talking and I allowed his words to sink in.

'Party room?' They briefly talked. Zack looked at me and started to walk. I matched his pace and proceeded to walk down the corridor with him.

"Now back to this party room."

"I believe that you will enjoy it." Zack giggled.

"What, an orgy room?" I aggressively said stopping in my tracks.

"Yes!"

"Hell nah! You got me fucked up! I don't know who the fuck you think I am, but I am not that bitch!" I barked getting the attention of a passing guest.

Zack wasn't about to cross examine me because he knew that I had my pistol ready and I was willing to use it. Zack looked down at my purse and noticed my hand was just inches away. "Now what you are going to do Zack, is take me to a secluded room for your more prestigious guest." He looked as if he wanted to speak his mind but like a good soldier, he took orders.

Zack escorted me to the room that I was in last night with Money. I entered the room looking around remembering the previous events. I had visions of Money fucking the girl in the chair and of me spanking the girl. As crazy as it sounds, the room was comfortable. I went over to the bed and had a seat. Zack just stared at me waiting for me to speak. I crossed my legs and set my purse next to me.

"Anything else miss?"

"Yes, bring me a couple to entertain me." I said like a boss bitch.

"Any couple?"

"Yes, any couple that is willing to put on a show for a few grand. Make sure that it's a male and female. None of that weird shit."

"I sure will."

"Oh and Zack, don't get cute and think that I don't have somebody watching Shaniqua. You try me and you will find her body in Lake Erie somewhere." I said meaning every word.

"I won't do that. Everything will go as planned."

"Sounds good to me. Now can you please send me my entertainment."

"Will do!" Zack said walking through the curtains.

Minutes later, an Asian couple came through the curtains followed by the waitress with the bad attitude. She brought me a bottle of champagne on ice and three champagne glasses. She sat them down and I gave her a tip. The couple didn't say a word to me and proceeded like I wasn't in the room. The waitress filled all three glasses and exited the room.

The couple was having sex right before me. The man had the lady's back pressed up against the wall as he thrusted inside her. The show wasn't arousing me, but their words were. I didn't know what they were saying to each other, but it sounded good. The lady was taking the dick and the man was giving her all he had. His little ass was working on that pussy. I sat back and closed my eyes imagining my "Asian sex toy" Anna sucking on my pussy. I laid back on the bed with my legs in the air and played with my pussy violently. I worked my fingers across the tip of my clit like I was a DJ mixing and scratching at a night club. I managed to peek my eyes open before I had an orgasm and the man was eating her pussy causing her to make all sorts of wild animal noises.

Suddenly, all of the lights turned off in the room. The only light that could be seen was the light from the "EXIT" sign in bright red letters. The couple started panicking and grabbing their clothing from the floor. I hopped up from the bed mad as hell that I didn't finish, but I had a job to do. This was Zack's signal. I pulled my gun from my purse and hurried out of the room. Using the lights from the emergency exit signs to guide me, I was able to find my way to the security office. I stood in front of the door trying hard to search for the key that Zack dropped in my purse. I wished that I would have cleaned my purse before I came in.

After scrambling through my purse for what seemed like hours which were only seconds, I finally found the key. I put it in the metal lock and turned the key. I felt the pressure from the door release and the door was unlocked. I put my shoulder against the door and eased it open. The lights in the building suddenly came back on and my stealth was no more. I rushed inside and grabbed the first person that I saw. I grabbed a man that was watching the cameras and placed the gun to his head.

"Don't nobody fucking move!" I shouted, pulling the man with me towards the red tubs of cash.

"You must be crazy coming in here with a gun," Money's momma added.

"I sure am!" I answered.

From the corner of my eye, I saw a trash can that was the perfect size to store all of this money. I didn't plan how I was going to take the money out once I had it, so this had to do. "Now you empty that trash can over there! Put all of the trash on the floor and put the cash into the bag!" I shouted pointing the gun at the other man that was watching the cameras.

He did what I ordered. He picked up three tubs filled with cash and emptied the money into the trash bag. I snatched the money from his grasp. I pushed the man that I was holding hostage onto the floor where a few loose dollars lay. He slipped on a few dollar bill piles and fell awkwardly on his shoulder causing him immediate pain.

"Now give me the video from tonight and last night!" I ordered, waving the gun around the room.

"Why do you need the video?" Money's mom asked.

"Bitch, don't ask me no fucking questions! You just worry about not getting killed tonight!"

The two men frantically looked for the video that I requested. I thought that they were going to hand me some DVDs but instead they handed me a flash drive. I waited while they put tonight's footage on the flash drive. I took the flash drives and dropped them into my purse. They both looked scared to death. I dug my hands in the trash bag and took out a hand full of cash and tipped the men for their services. I carefully backed out into the hallway keeping my aim on them. I shut the door and headed for my exit.

Rapidly I walked down the corridor and my eyes fall upon a familiar face. I stopped moving and waited for the man to approach me. He casually walked like I had all fucking day. He was walking like he had something in his shoe and brushing his long thick beard.

"Treasure is that you?" He said coming closer.

The face that I recognized was Redd. Brian's rap artist. Last time I saw him was in the studio, when he was bragging about going on tour with some half naked women. Why was he here?

"Redd? What are you doing here?" I asked giving him a friendly hug. The trash bag swung and hit him in the leg.

"What do you mean, what am I doing here? What are you doing here?" He asked frowning his face.

"I have a girlfriend that works in here. I was here for a little support. It's her first night."

"Really? Who is she? Maybe you can introduce me."

"Redd where is my husband?" I questioned looking him up and down. "He isn't in one of these rooms now is he?"

"Treasure, now you know Brian ain't about to be out here like that. He's probably in the room waiting for you to call him."

"What hotel is he in?" I said walking away from him.

"The Hyatt."

"Well I am about to pay my man a visit. Please don't ever tell him about seeing me in here. You understand?"

"Yes ma'am."

Redd and the rest of the artists knew about my past street life. Shit, most of the mutha fuckas in Columbus knew. The streets talked and my name was known to handle business out here. Most of them were well aware of my brother's reputation in these streets so crossing me was highly unlikely. But if anyone did, they knew what the final result would be.

I continued to walk towards the exit and right past Zack. He looked at the bag, but he didn't utter a word. I pushed opened the door and walked out with a trash bag full of money and a couple of flash drives for added insurance. Looking behind me, I saw Money's mom and the rest of them creeps out of the security room. I laughed as I headed for my car. She was screaming for security, but little did she know that I had the security working for me.

Inside the car, I called Shaniqua. She said that Money came over soon after I had left. Shaniqua said she'd opened the door wearing nothing but her birthday suit and they did the damn thing. She started to give me details about their sex session and I had to cut her off. I mean, I thought he was a weird freaky mutha fucka. But, this woman was saying some shit that I couldn't imagine. She said that he fucked her in the ass. She said Money had his fingers in her ass as he fucked her doggy-style. What topped it all off, she said that she gave him a show by fucking a wine bottle and squirting out the wine from her pussy. Way too much information! I had to throw in the towel with hearing about her exciting night. On the flip side, she said that they sat and talked about the upcoming court date and he agreed to let her keep her ring and car if she just signed over her rights. While she was talking to me about it, I almost believed that she was considering the idea of signing her rights over. I had to end the call because the bitch was getting on my nerves. I couldn't stand a stupid bitch; especially when it came to her kids. Before I ended the call, I told her that I would swing by her house and give her- her cut of the cash. She was excited.

On the way to Shaniqua's house, I was wondering how much money I took from the club. I decided to stop at a nearby supercenter and count the cash in the parking lot. I turned the trash bag upside down and poured out the cash on the passenger floor. I started picking out the hundred dollar bills first then the fifties and so on. I ended up counting $135,000 thousand dollars and I still had a few more bills to count. The extra dollars wasn't more than about two or three hundred dollars. I expected a little more, but I was more than happy for Money's contribution to Brian's birthday fund.

After counting up the money, I took out thirty thousand for Shaniqua's cut of the pie. She should be happy with being paid thirty bands for opening her legs to a man whom she had to numerous times before. Shit, thirty bands for any one night of sex was well worth it. She needed the money and in my opinion, she needed the dick more. That amount of cash should be enough to get her a good lawyer that would fight for her rights and give her full custody.

I parked my car next door to Shaniqua's house right in front of the old couple's home. It was two in the morning, so I knew that they were sound to sleep. I climbed out and headed for her front door. A bright motion light popped on above her garage as I made my way for the door. I knocked on her door, but she didn't answer. I thought that maybe Money put her ass to sleep with some good dick. I went back to the window that I was snooping in earlier, but noticed not one light was on in the house. I stepped back to the front of the house and pulled out my phone and called the sistah again. Again no answer.

I climbed back inside of my car and patiently waited for Shaniqua's arrival. I couldn't stop looking at the time on my phone. Brian called but yet again, I ignored him. I figured he was all alone in the room waiting for my call. Where could she be? I tried to relax by turning on some music, but that didn't help. The music actually put me more on edge. I pulled out a pack of Trident gum from my purse and I must have eaten four pieces before I noticed a car slowing down a few houses up the street. The car head lights were beaming in my direction; damn near blinding me. I turned off the car and sunk down in the seat barely able to look out of the windshield. Just as I thought, the car slowly pulled into Shaniqua's driveway. I managed to prop myself on my center console to get a better view without revealing my identity. The car belonged to Money. The paint shined from the motion light. I had a clear view of him and his passenger. Shaniqua stepped out of his car wearing a pair of bleached jeans and a red corset showing off her boobs. Money didn't even give the girl a chance to fully get to her door before he put the car in reverse and started blasting his music. I watched him looking back as he pulled ou,t but he didn't even notice me. I waited until his lights disappeared from my sight before I opened my door.

Shaniqua opened the door shocked to see me. The scent of my pearberry lotion ran up to my nose reminding me that I had left it in her guest room. I had her money in my purse and the pistol in my hand. She barely had the door open as I easily forced myself in. She didn't say a word and just looked at me with disbelief. I walked right past her and made my way to the bar in her kitchen. I didn't realize that I was sitting in the chair that she was being fucked in earlier until I had taken a seat and poured myself a glass of wine.

"Treasure, what's up girl? Did you really do it?" She asked pouring herself a glass.

"Didn't I tell you that I was going to do it? Here's your cut like I had promised," I said pulling out the cash and neatly stacking it on the bar.

"Oh, thank you!" She said cheerfully.

Over the next ten minutes, Shaniqua and I talked. Shaniqua didn't hesitate to tell me about the rest of her night. I was sipping from my glass waiting to hear the bullshit from her lips. I felt like she owed me an explanation for making me wait on her. Then suddenly she just stopped in the middle of her story.

"What's wrong girl?" I asked sitting down my glass.

"Treasure… I made it all up." Shaniqua cried.

"What?" I asked confused.

"Money didn't want to fuck me. He looked at me like I was a dirty whore from the street.

'Well bitch…'

"I'm sure he didn't," I managed to say trying to control myself from laughing.

"I tried to give it to him and he didn't want it. The man didn't even let me suck his dick. What man turns down head?"

I just studied her facial expressions. The girl was clearly hurt. Shit, I wondered why did he turn down some pussy or head for that matter. Money was a freak. He ate my pussy not knowing me from shit. *'Why didn't he take the bait?'*

"I'm sorry…I'm sorry," she sobbed.

"Sorry for what?" I questioned picking my glass back up.

"Um…"

"What?" I asked concerned.

"Never mind it's nothing," she said taking a gulp from her glass. I noticed her trying to avoid eye contact.

"Just say it girl."

"For telling you that bogus story. I didn't want you thinking that he wasn't attracted to me. I know that he wants you because you wouldn't be here."

"No honey. He doesn't want me. He wants my pussy. I am a happily married woman with a man waiting on me at home. Money would never have me. Shit, he won't ever see me again. What y'all need to do is work out the parental situation for y'all son and both move on."

"Right!" She said drying her face. "That's exactly what we started talking about."

Shaniqua said that Money and her rode around the city discussing the whole reason why they had separated. She believed that he was having a change of heart and maybe wanted to get his family back together. I had to wake her up from her fantasy and bring her back to earth. The reality was that Money wanted to stick his dick in everybody and could care less about her. I even tried to influence her to take the money and just leave. She toyed with the Orlando idea, but I could tell that she wasn't serious.

Suddenly her phone rang. She got up from her seat and rushed toward the sound. I figured that she was running for some dick; either Zack or Money. When I came into the kitchen, I noticed her purse sitting on the counter next to the refrigerator. I climbed down from my seat and hurried to her purse. To my surprise, her purse was opened for anyone to see. I opened it a little further apart and there was my bottle of lotion along with a box of condoms and a bottle of medicine. At least the girl practiced safe sex. The box was missing a condom. The box contained three condoms and one was missing. I wondered if she just kept boxes of condoms for unplanned moments. I normally hide one in my purse, but I haven't had sex with another man in years. Being nosy, I picked up the pill bottle and read the name listed on the medication and it was hers. I heard the sounds of her heels slapping against her wood floors coming closer. I quickly put her bottle back in her purse and walked back to my seat. I remembered that I left my bottle of lotion in her purse, but I had proceeded to my seat.

Shaniqua entered the kitchen giggling like I had told her a joke.

"What's up?" I asked crossing my legs and taking another sip.

"That was Zack. He told me about the reaction at the club," she answered.

"Money is going to be pissed when he finds out," I added.

"Right!"

We both laughed.

Shaniqua and I continued to talk for another hour and a half. We discussed everything from my relationship with Brian to hers with both Money and Zack. I wasn't surprised to hear that Zack asked her to marry him. That man was pussy whipped more than any man that I have ever known. He was willing to die for somebody that he didn't have kids with or a real commitment to. Crazy if you ask me but hey, that's what love does to folks.

We finished our drinks and she walked me towards the door. Shaniqua gave me a hug and again thanked me for the money. She stated that I didn't have to get back on the highway this late and could stay with her, but I gently declined her invite. Just by the look on her face, I knew that she wanted to taste my goodies and I wasn't falling for it. She claimed that she was concerned for my safety; especially after sharing a bottle of Moscato wine with her. I couldn't lie, I was feeling good. The drinks from the club and the full glass of wine had me buzzing, but I wasn't too fucked up to stay.

I opened the door and stepped out causing the motion light to turn on. I found it strange that she didn't ask about the club footage that I had taken out of the security room. She seemed liked that was important to her earlier, but maybe it slipped her mind while she was trying to fuck Money.

CHAPTER 7

During my drive to the hotel where Brian was staying, I couldn't help but feel so alive. I didn't know that reverting to my past ways would make me feel so good. I couldn't stop smiling and singing every song that blasted through my speakers. People were pulling up next to me laughing and staring at me at red lights. They were barely woke or ready to go to sleep. They didn't understand my joy, but I knew where it came from. Shit, I wished I would have done this a long time ago. Taking this man's money was better than having some good ass sweaty sex. All I needed to add to my joy was my husband's strong hands on my body.

When I arrived at the hotel, it was close to six in the morning. I had to stop and get gas, plus I knew how my man loved breakfast in bed. The hotel food would be nice to order for him, but Brian was a food critic. His physique said it all. Brian loved the pancakes and omelets at IHOP. I ordered us both some breakfast from the restaurant and picked up the order shortly after. The carry-out line was unbelievably long considering the time of day, but it was well worth it for my 'fat man.'

The hotel valet helped me out of my car and grabbed my suitcase full of clothes and money. I looked at him crazy, but I knew that he was just doing his job. I took my food from the car. The food scent was filling the air and I was eager to get in the room and eat. I grabbed my suitcase from the man and started for the door. The valet man stood there holding his hand out and I had forgotten that I had took the keys out of the ignition. I handed the man the keys, but he continued to stand still staring me down. I tipped the man a twenty-dollar bill and proceeded to the front entrance. I felt his eyes undressing me. I smiled, loving the attention of a good looking young man. He looked as if he was in his early twenties.

I entered through the glass sliding doors and it seemed as if all eyes were on me. Two older white gentleman wearing business suits sat in the lobby. The older of the two was reading a newspaper sipping on some coffee when I first stepped in, but he removed the paper from his view and looked in my direction. The other man was a good looking Italian man with a clean trimmed beard. He looked like an underwear model. He had an athletic body that would resemble an Olympic swimmer or track star. His suit was fly also. He wore it with confidence. Although he was cute as hell and sexy as fuck, I couldn't help but notice the ring on his ring finger. The man was taken and so was I. I giggled with the thought.

Approaching the front desk, I noticed the hosts whispering amongst themselves. I sit my purse on top of the counter and asked for Brian's room number. The host couldn't help himself from staring directly at my boobs. I mean, he wasn't trying to be discreet with it either. I had to clear my throat just to get his eyes from my cleavage to his computer. I told him that I had just gotten into town and wanted to give my husband breakfast in bed. Again, he looked me up and down then he asked for my identification. I was glad to show him proof of my identity. I had changed my name from my old married name soon after we were married. I couldn't wait to get Rashad's name off of all of my paper work. Occasionally, I would still get mail with my old name, but that was far in-between. The host insisted on calling Brian, but I used my charm to make him think otherwise. I told the host a little bit of the truth about my plan with Brian. He stood listening; licking his lips like he was Chris Brown continuing to tittie fuck me with his eyes. When I finished, he handed me over my key to the room and I stepped away.

I found the elevators and I stepped towards them trying to catch the next one. The nice looking Italian man joined me. We both stood in front of the elevators waiting for the next one to arrive. He was drooling all over me like the host, but I managed to catch his eye a few times. He had me blushing like a young girl in high school. The elevator door rang and the elevator in front of him opened. He signaled for me to enter the elevator first. I walked right pass him and pushed "7"; the floor which Brian was staying on. I stepped to the back of the elevator and leaned against the wall. He pushed his floor and stood on the opposite side of me. I looked at the glowing numbers for the different floors and noticed he didn't pick a floor.

'He was on the same floor as Brian and I.'

"That food sure does smell good," he said.

"I hope it is good. I am so hungry," I giggled.

"It looks like a lot of food. Is all of that for you?"

"Oh no! It's for me and my husband," I answered.

'Damn that just slipped out.'

"Damn, he's a lucky man!" He said shaking his head checking me out.

I laughed.

"I'm sorry. My name is Giovanni. And yours?" He said in a deep Italian dialect.

"My name is Treasure."

The doors opened and the elevator doorbell rang again.

"After you Mrs. Treasure."

"Thank you."

I knew that his eyes were taking the last images of my ass. He would soon see it again. So, I gave him a model walk that was so mean that I made myself laugh. He was going to remember this ass.

"Mrs. Treasure, I see that you are a pretty and professional looking woman. If you are ever shopping for any commercial real estate, don't be afraid to call me," he said handing me his business card.

His card had his office number and cell number on it; along with a cute picture of him. I was definitely going to call him, but not for what he thought. It was time for me to lick a white collar man for his riches and he could be my number one draft pick. His bank account might be double the amount of Money's and I needed to make a withdrawal.

I took his number and turned opposite directions down the corridor. Not even two steps away from the elevator, I can hear a man's moans and groans. The sounds seemed to echo like they were being played through surround sound speakers. I continued to walk but my attention was stuck on the sounds.

"Damn Redd! What the fuck are you doing?" I spat furious from the sight.

"Treasure?"

"Get your mutha fucking ass out of here Redd! If security catches you, it will make the whole company look bad."

"You're right."

Redd shoved his dick back into his pants and stood up. The girl backed away from him, but I knew exactly what she was doing. While he was fixing his clothing, I was staring this girl up and down. I couldn't forget her face. And she knew it also. She tried to keep from giving me eye contact by looking down at the floor. She was standing there quiet as hell. This was the same chic that was raising hell at Zack earlier at the club. Ratchet as hell, now you want to play shy. Bitch, get the fuck out of here! You're embarrassed because I caught your groupie ass on your knees giving head. From the sounds Redd was making, you were doing the damn thang.

"Why are you out here?" I questioned looking him up and down.

"We couldn't make it to the room," he laughed.

"You are nasty."

"You have a little nasty girl in you too. Don't act like that."

"Redd…" I was cut off.

"Treasure, you don't have to say anymore. We are going to the room."

"I appreciate it."

Redd, the girl and myself walked past a few guest rooms until we reached ours. Redd was right next door to Brian. I could only imagine the shit that they were about to do. Redd opened his door and allowed her in first. When she stepped in he gave her a slap on the ass and followed right behind her. I couldn't help but laugh at his goofy ass. Redd was always into something. He kind of reminded me of my brother.

I quietly put the key card in the door and gently pushed it open when the green light turned on. I crept into the room and softly closed the door back. I skillfully maneuvered my body into the room without banging my suitcase against the door alarming him. I stepped in a little more and sat my suitcase against the wall along with my purse. I made sure that it was positioned correctly so that it wouldn't fall.

I proceeded further into the hotel room and I finally saw Brian. A familiar scent hit me in the face. I couldn't master the scent, but I knew the smell very well. I sat the food down at a business desk along with my keys. I took out each container of food continuing to use my ninja skills of silence. The food remained to be warm and I was ready to dive in. But, I was going to give my husband some lovin' first.

Brian was lied back on the bed knocked out. He was only wearing a pair of socks and boxers. His dick head was poking out from the slit of his boxers. I thought about waking him up to some good head but feeding my empty stomach was more important.

The tour must have really taken a lot of energy out of him. I noticed a half empty champagne bottle next to the bed along with his cell phone and wallet. I figured he must have drunk himself to sleep. The television was on his favorite sports channel with the remote resting on his tattooed stomach. I picked up the champagne bottle and replaced it with his meal.

I finished eating watching the highlights from the night's top plays. I was addicted to watching sports also. Again, I thought to wake him by giving him some head or sitting on his lap and rubbing his dick between my pussy lips to get him fully erect. The thought alone made me wet. I slid out of my dress and allowed it to dance off my body to the floor. I stepped out of the dress and approached Brian. I went to his side of the bed and squatted down bending my knees. I had his penis staring directly at me. I took my index and middle finger between my thighs and begun to scroll my finger over my clit. My pussy began smacking instantly. With his right leg hanging half-way off the bed I was in a perfect position to give him the best head of his dreams. I gently grabbed his penis and removed it out of his boxers. The scent became noticeably stronger. Not a second longer, I recognized the scent. The scent smelt just like my pearberry lotion. I know that this fool didn't jack off to my lotion. I wondered if he snuck a bottle out of my closet.

A sense of guilt came over me. My husband didn't go out with his artists to Money's freaky club because he wanted to have phone sex with me again. The fucked up part about it was that I left him hanging. I had a damn good man. A loyal man. He could have been caught in the hallway fucking one of these groupies but instead, he jacked himself to sleep.

I was going to make this night right by him. Just giving him some head wasn't going to be enough. He deserved the full course. I stood up from my bent position and smiled looking at his penis. His penis was like cake to a fat kid for me.

Suddenly, I heard a soft knock at the door. I was frozen wondering who would come to Brian's room this time of day. The thought made me furious. Without taking a second thought, I stomped over towards the door ready to go the fuck off.

Knock. Knock.

I swung the door open violently and there the mutha fucka stood; Redd.

"What you want fool?" I said aggressively but managing to keep my voice down.

"Damn Treasure!" Redd said checking me out.

I forgot that I was naked when I had taken off for the door. Embarrassed, I stepped behind the door and covered my breasts with my free arm.

"You know what time it is?"

"Now, I see what time it is. Brian is the fucking man!" Redd said with excitement.

I giggled.

Redd started looking down at his door and back at me. I poked my head out and the waitress was also in the doorway wrapped in a sheet. She managed to lift her hand up and wave hi at me. I just shook my head and turned my attention back at him.

"Well I don't want to hold you guys up. I was just wondering if y'all had an extra condom for me?" Redd looked at me like he was pleading from inside.

"Redd, you mean to tell me that you brought that girl to your room and you don't have a condom?" I said sarcastically.

"Umm…"

"You must don't want the pussy."

"Shit…"

"Well I can't help you. Goodnight!"

After closing the door, I decided to take a shower. I wanted my body to be nice and clean for my man. I felt like I had been in that dress all damn night long. Although the nice breeze kept me from sweating down there, I wasn't going to dare put my pussy on my man's dick if it wasn't clean enough to eat.

I entered the bathroom and it was amazingly beautiful. The bathroom looked like a five-star spa. I sat my body soap and deodorant on the counter and turned the shower water on. The water pressure was blasting the water hard against the wall causing a loud thumping noise. I quickly turned the water down with hopes that sound didn't wake Brian.

I wasn't in the shower long; due to the fact that I wanted to sneak back into the room and make love to my man. I climbed out of the shower and remembered that I didn't have my lotion bottle. The image of my lotion in Shaniqua's purse crossed my mind. I patted my body dry looking over at the counter for a substitute to keep my body soft and smelling good. Luckily, the hotel had complimentary toiletries for guests. I grabbed the hotel bottle of lotion and applied it to my body. Almost slipping on the floor, I took a spare towel and laid it on the floor where water puddle had formed. I placed my foot on top of the toilet seat and began to rub the lotion on my legs and ass. I pushed my hand down towards my ankles to lotion my feet and I noticed a gold wrapper in the trashcan under the sink. Normally I wouldn't pay it any mind, but the object seemed to stick out. I pulled the trash can further out away from the shadows. I reached my hand inside of the trash can which only had this item in it and pulled it out. To my surprise, the gold wrapper was what I believed it to be.

A Magnum condom.

I'm not stupid to believe that this was by mistake or that the housekeeper didn't clean the room before Brian brought his fat ass in here. I was just wondering what bitch did he have the balls to fuck while I was out putting my life on the line to get him a fucking birthday gift.

I exited the bathroom and went directly for my suitcase. Tears blurred my vision. The tears ran down my face like a steady stream. My heart was racing 100 miles per hour. I could feel my blood boiling through my veins as my temperature continued to rise with each step closer to my suitcase. I was going to make this cheating mutha fucka feel my pain. I gave him my heart and trust. I never wanted to allow a man close to my heart again after my first husband, Rashad but I let down my guard. He was going to feel this pain that I was feeling.

I unzipped my bag fully causing my clothes and the bag full of money to fall to the floor. I didn't care about making any noise anymore. Shit, the last sound he would be hearing is the sound of my gun blasting him in the head. The problem for me was that my gun was in my purse. I knew that I wasn't thinking straight, but I had to do this. I felt disrespected and dirty; something to the feeling Shaniqua had with Money.

With the gun in my hand, I cocked it back and began to approach him. Brian continued to sleep like a baby. He remained in the same position as he was when I left for the shower. I went right back to where I was when I was thinking of giving him some head. I stood over him; reminiscing on all of the good times we had. I tried to erase the thoughts so that I could squeeze the trigger. It seemed like my trigger finger wouldn't move. My hand started shaking like an old lady. I wasn't nervous; just hurt.

Suddenly, I heard the ringing of my cell phone. The phone which I used to communicate with Money and Shaniqua had a different ringtone. This ring was coming from my personal cell phone. I wondered who would be calling me first thing in the morning, but I decided to get it anyway. The sounds were disturbing Brian which caused him to toss in his sleep, but I didn't care. I pulled the phone from my purse and noticed my mother's name across the screen.

"Hello," I said into the receiver answering the phone.

"Mom it's me," Raymond said.

"What are you doing up this early Raymond," I asked walking back into the bathroom.

I picked up the condom wrapper from the counter top and balled it up in my hand.

"I was worried about you mom. You told me that you would be home by last night."

'Damn that boy didn't forget shit.'

"I will be home by early tomorrow afternoon."

"Okay mom. I was just worried about you."

"That's so sweet. I am alright. In fact, I am here with Brian now."

"Well, that makes me feel a whole lot better mom."

I laughed.

I continued to talk to Raymond for another minute or so. He was always worried about me when I went out alone. I believed he had a feeling that I would one day not come back like his father. Although Raymond is old enough to talk to about most things, the topic of his father never came out. I almost believed he knew the truth, but I would take the truth with me to my grave. My son would be devastated to find out that I was behind the murder of his father. That, I couldn't stomach and it was something that I was going to have to live with.

After ending my call with my son, I had mixed feelings about killing Brian. I sat at the desk looking him over; deciding on my next move. Being a cheater was bad, but not enough to kill him. I had to take control of my emotions. Besides, I was always going to do me. I just wanted an honest relationship with my husband. What I did was strictly business. Even fucking with Anna was business. I was going to use Anna's body to please Brian and myself. The thought of another man's touch didn't appeal to me. Although Money did his thang, I wasn't going to ruin my relationship over some mutha fucka that could eat the fuck out of some pussy. I knew what I had at home and I cherished that. I got up from the chair and stuffed the gun back into my purse. The nice gentleman that I met in the elevator business' card flipped over in my purse. I played with the thought of repaying Brian back by going down to the nice man's room and putting it on him, but I decided otherwise. I was thinking like a hoe. I needed a real explanation for this. There was clear evidence of him fucking somebody in here. I had to clear my mind.

I took the champagne bottle and tilted it upside down pouring the rest of the champagne on him. The champagne splashed him right in the face. Brian hopped up from the bed, not knowing what was going on. He looked as if he was drowning and gasping for his last breath.

"Treasure, what the fuck are you doing?" Brian shouted awakening from his sleep.

"No, what the fuck are you doing!" I shouted from the top of my lungs. He looked at me in dismay and I couldn't form the words to express what I was feeling. I had the condom wrapper in my hand so I crumbled it up in my hand and threw it at him.

Brian acted as if he didn't know what I had threw at him, but he knew it was serious. Tears rolled down my face as I stood waiting for an explanation. He unraveled the foiled wrapper and read the bold black letter. He looked back up to me and understood my fury.

"Tiana that's not mine!"

I remained silent. I shook my head not able to believe that this man in front of me was cheating but more importantly, lying about it.

"Tiana…Baby please believe me." Brian pleaded causing his voice to crack.

"What am I supposed to think Brian? I drove all of the way here to surprise you and you turn around and surprise me with this?" I said snatching the condom wrapper from his hand and throwing it somewhere in the room.

"I swear it's not mine," he said softly.

"Then whose is it then Brian?" I questioned smacking my lips with a lot of attitude.

"Listen babe. I first need you to calm down and take a seat."

"Sit down for what? What do I need to sit down for?"

"Listen, I know where the condom might have come from."

"I'm listening," I said sarcastically.

"Tonight everyone wanted to go out and they asked me but I refused. Redd said that he was going to send me some company. I agreed to the idea because I didn't think he was going to actually go through with it."

"Well?"

"Well, he sent me an escort. The lady came in and insisted for me to fuck her, but I declined."

"Come on now Brian! You are sitting here lying through your mutha fucking teeth. If you fucked the bitch just say that you did so we can move on with it."

"I didn't fuck her. I promise."

"Ain't no man going to turn down any pussy that's right in front of him," I added shaking my head with disbelief.

"Honestly, the woman came in here ready to fuck me. I believe Redd paid her a hell of a lot of money to do what she did."

"What the fuck did she do?" I asked curiously.

"The woman came in wearing a trench coat and soon as she got next to the desk she dropped her coat to the floor. The woman was totally naked. I mean, I didn't even get her name by this time. She only said that she was sent by a friend. I knew then that this was who Redd was talking about."

"Was she cute?" I asked waiting to hear his response.

"She was alright. Not much ass, but some big chocolate titties."

"You liked them titties didn't you?" I asked carefully watching his facial expressions.

Brian knew that he could talk to me about this woman because we shared these types of conversations all of the time. We would be watching television and I would just come out and ask him would he fuck the lady on the television and he would answer. He would do the same to me but never asked about me fucking another man; it was always a woman. We both would also check out women together; walking in the mall, at the movies, at the club, shit - wherever women were. It was our little thing.

"You know I am an ass man baby."

"Don't baby me fool. I need to hear the rest of this story," I said pushing away his hands as he attempted to rub my thighs. I remembered that I was naked and he wasn't going to get any. So, I walked over to my suitcase and put on some panties and a T-shirt.

"Where are you going?" he asked.

"Just finish the damn story!" I ordered, pulling my panties over my hips. I chose to wear a pair of thongs just so I could tease him with all of this ass.

"She sat her purse down and pulled out a bottle of lotion. She looked at me and smiled before bending over showing me her pussy. She then put her leg up on the chair and asked me to rub some lotion on her."

"And your dumb ass did," I said sucking my teeth.

"I did," he answered looking down to the floor.

"Stupid! I know that wasn't it."

"Well she turned some music on her phone and started doing a little dance. I thought the girl was a stripper and wanted to give me a private show. She started dancing on me putting her tits all in my face and grinding her ass on my dick. The dance wasn't doing shit for me honestly. The chic couldn't dance at all. I went to reach for a few loose bills in my pants to tip her for trying and she tugged at my pants pulling them down to my knees."

"Brian look at me. You mean to tell me that this bitch over powered your big ass? Stop it!" I looked at him with disbelief. His story sounded so bogus to me.

"I mean she didn't over power me, but she made sure that my pants didn't come back up. She wrapped her legs around my waist and started working. I was caught off guard."

I laughed. "Caught off guard."

"I was! I pushed her off of me and when I did, she scratched me with the heel of her shoe. She got off me and went to get a wet towel to stop the bleeding. Then suddenly she took my dick in her mouth."

I sat silently. If I was in my right mind, I would have slapped the shit out of him. But, I wanted to hear the rest of this bullshit for some reason and it was keeping me from reacting how I truly wanted. I knew that a man was only going to do what his body really wanted to do. My brother told me that when I was still in high school.

"And?"

"And she continued to suck my dick for about five minutes. Before I was ready to nut she stopped sucking on me and went over to her coat. I noticed that she pulled her belt from her coat. It dragged across the floor as she gave me this model walk toward me. I didn't know what she was going to do next. She got right there and took off her heels and jumped back on me. My dick was right against her pussy so I pulled her towards me. She laughed like she was enjoying me being physical with her. She then covered my eyes with the belt and went back down to suck me off. When my man was fully hard, she tried to sit on it reverse cowgirl style."

"What?" I questioned like I was anticipating on hearing something different.

"Exactly! I ripped off the belt from my head and hopped up. She said that Redd paid her to do the whole nine yards," he said raising his voice like he was angered.

"That shit still don't explain the condom wrapper in the bathroom if y'all were out here."

"Oh, I went in the bathroom to shower and she came in with the condom ready. She said that she didn't know if I wanted to use condoms or some dumb shit."

"No! What some dumb shit is having the bitch in your room! Then on top of that when she started acting thirsty to fuck your ass, you should have thrown her thot ass out! I swear you can be so damn gullible at times." I shouted feeling my blood pressure rising again. I placed my hand over my chest. It felt as if my heart was about to burst.

"Tiana, are you okay?" Brian said reaching for me, but I slapped his arms down.

"Fuck you! You could have just told the truth!"

"I did!"

"Then why does your balls still smell like that bitches pussy then?" I said staring him down like a wolf that's ready to attack.

"Umm…"

"While you're thinking of another mutha fucking lie, let me go next door and show my mutha fucking appreciating to Redd."

Brian rushed me at the door before I had a chance to show Redd how I get down. I wouldn't have killed the man because he wasn't the one sticking his dick in a bitch. But, he was going to see how good my hands were.

Brian and I argued more into the wee hours of the morning until we both eventually had enough and went to sleep. I fell asleep sitting up at the desk. I would be damned to lay in bed with him for a while. I was going to put him on pussy restrictions like no other man had ever been on. Soon as we arrive at home, he was going to go get tested although he claimed that he didn't fuck her. I knew better. He wasn't going to feel the wrath of his actions until he saw Anna and I going hard in the bed without his nasty ass. That was a gift to give a dog.

CHAPTER 8

I had to set my alarm for noon although I just gotten to the house four hours ago. Brian knew that after hearing his lame ass story that he had to do what he had to in order to keep me happy. Brian started off by taking the trip with me instead of riding back with his artists. He drove all of the way and he even suffered listening to my old school R & B. I acted as if I were a DJ skipping to my favorite jams. I honestly believe that he decided to be with me because he knew that I was going to fly off the handle on Redd's ass. I wanted to fuck Redd up or at least give him a piece of mind. Brian gladly opted to drive us back home with the thought on his mind. I didn't say much of anything to him because I was still upset. He knew it to, so he kept the chatter to a bare minimum and listened to the music.

When we arrived home, he thought after bringing our bags in that everything was cool. Fuck no! I ain't that fucking easy. And I wasn't ready to forgive. I took myself straight to the bedroom. I undressed myself purposely taking my clothes off slowly then I slid under the covers. I only took my eyes off of him for a second and he almost beat me at undressing. He was standing at his side of the bed unbuckling his Gucci belt and pulling his pants down. It was hard to resist the bulge in his boxer briefs, but his ass had to pay for my pain and suffering. He started taking off his shirt and then his jewelry. I heard the metal of his chains drop onto the nightstand and then his cell phone. I rolled over facing the sliding doors to the balcony trying hard to be a bitch and not to give in. Brian bounced his big ass on the bed and climbed under the covers. I immediately felt his body heat getting closer. He inched himself closer tugging the covers towards him which triggered my attitude. I pulled back the covers and I smacked my lips. This fool laughed under his breath, but loud enough to catch my attention. He ignored my attitude and continued to inch closer putting his manhood between my ass cheeks. I scooted forward and so did he. He placed his hand on my hip and began to kiss my back smoothly. His touch was needed, but I managed to keep my control not allowing my feelings to get into his persuasive touch. He brushed his hand up my side sneaking his fingers to my bare breasts. I shot him back a vicious frown and shrugged my shoulder taking his finger away from my body.

"Baby I am so sorry," he said with a soft tone of voice.

I closed my eyes allowing his words to sink in. I allowed my mind to be the judge of his words. My heart struggled to stay caged up like a mad man, but my mouth worked faster than my mind and heart. "Well, take your sorry ass to the other room." I said simply meaning every word.

"Damn! We can't make up?"

"I'm unsure of that yet! Maybe when you feel like telling the truth.

"Close the door behind you Brian. I have to get up in a few hours," I said watching him walk out the door with a fully erect soldier.

"That's fucked up Tiana."

"Oh, here's your pillow. Cuddle up with that," I added throwing his pillow at him.

Brian walked out and I went straight to sleep.

My alarm woke me up. The time read 12:00 on my cell phone. I struggled to get out of the bed, but I knew that I had a lot to do. I turned my body toward the other side of the bed and to my surprise Brian didn't try to creep back into the bed while I was sleep. He must have really felt the heat I was giving him. I pulled away my covers and rushed for the bathroom. I had to pee badly. I was so mad last night that I had forgotten to use the bathroom when I came home. I washed up and brushed my teeth. While brushing my teeth, my stomach began to growl like it was talking to me. It had been hours since I last ate. I decided to make myself a huge breakfast to end my hunger.

I pulled off my panties throwing them in the dirty clothes hamper and threw on a Self Made T-shirt. My phone began to chime, but I was so hungry that I didn't even check to see who was calling. I grabbed the phone and rushed down to the kitchen.

Walking through the living room, I noticed Brian sleeping on the couch all curled up with his pillow. He looked so innocent but he wasn't. He had dirt on his hands and was going to work hard to get them clean before they would touch me again.

My phone continued to chime as I started pulling out ingredients from the refrigerator and kitchen cabinets. After the second missed call, it was bothering me so I answered noticing that the caller was Anna. I was excited to hear her voice. I continued cooking while I talked to her.

Anna was driving on her way to our house. She was calling to remind me of our meeting that I planned. Nothing formal, just some girl time and I deserved it. The stress that Brian put on me and the lick that I hit on Money was taking away from my joy. I was normally always smiling and full of life. But, the thought of my man fucking some other bitch without my permission had my mind fucked up.

Knowing that Brian was awakened by the scent of the food, I began to talk to Anna about the whole night. I did this intentionally for him to hear me. I wanted him to really feel bad about his actions. Me talking to Anna about his cheating ass would embarrass the hell out of him. Like I thought, he got his ass up off the couch, entered the kitchen and just stared at me. His mean mug didn't bother me. I continued to talk as if he wasn't there.

Anna was in awe about the whole situation. She didn't know Brian well; just a few meetings at the dance studio when we had an event for the dancers. Anna sounded as if she was hurt to hear the news. Her voiced cracked hearing the words from my mouth. She shouted through the phone that she will be arriving sooner than I had thought. We were already about to meet, but now it was more about me. She was eager to come help me get over it. We decided that going to get some things for the trip would relieve some of this stress. Nothing like an excuse to do a little shopping.

Brian continued to give me this blank stare until I ended the call. I continued to ignore his ass and made my plate. I made enough food for the two of us, but I wasn't putting the idea in his head that the rest belonged to him. I had the steak sizzling on my plate like it was prepared at Apple Bee's. The steak had a little char perfectly cooked with green peppers, onions and mushrooms. To add to my plate, I had a baked potato hot out of the oven. I unraveled the foil from the potato and smothered it with cheese and broccoli. Brian leaned across the kitchen island licking his lips like I was going to make his plate. Normally, I would make his plate first and bring it to him but this fool was in the dog house. I purposely went over to the refrigerator and bent all the way over to show off my fatty as I took out the jug of orange juice. I looked over my shoulders and his eyes were right where I wanted them. On my ass.

Ring! Our security bell chimed. I walked over to the alarm and pushed the button for the gates to open and allow Anna in.

"Who's that?" Brian asked.

I didn't respond and took my seat at the breakfast nook and started cutting up my steak.

Seconds later the doorbell rings. "Get that honey!" I shouted at Brian swallowing a mouth full of food.

"What?" Brain shouted back aggressively.

Ring. Ring. The doorbell chimed.

"Don't fucking get it Brian! I will - damn!" I said storming off towards the door.

Brian was back at his seat on the couch in front of the television. I guess he got an attitude because I didn't make him a plate, but I didn't care.

I opened the door and Anna was standing in the doorway looking like a rich man's foreign wife. She was wearing cut up shorts showing off her curves and a see threw blouse. She had her blouse in a knot just above her navel showing off her stomach and piercing. Anna smiled when my eyes met hers. Her dimples were deep and sexy. She managed to buy a bottle of wine and flowers before coming over. I thought that was a really nice gesture. I invited her in with a hug and a soft kiss on her cheek. Anna also kissed me on the cheek. I felt the warm summer air crawling up my legs and between my thighs. I released her from my grasp and took the wine bottle from her hands. She stepped in, taking off her sunglasses revealing her pretty almond shaped eyes.

I closed the door behind her and started for the wine cooler in the kitchen. I told Anna to have a seat in the living room. She reluctantly waved at Brian. I could feel the tension in the air, so I broke the silence. "Anna, let's go up to my bedroom so I can get dressed."

"Alright," she responded getting back up to her feet.

"Tiana."

"Girl go ahead of me. My bedroom is the first room on the right. As a matter of fact, girl try to find something for me. I will be all day."

"No problem," she replied continuing to head for the stairs.

I waited for Anna to be out of sight and out of hearing distance to respond to him. "What Brian?"

"Um…"

I cut him off, "What Brian?"

"What's that all about?" He questioned looking confused.

"What? Anna?"

"Yeah!"

"Brian, you shouldn't even be thinking of sex. Didn't you get enough of that in Cleveland?" I said sarcastically.

"I told you, Tiana what happened. I am sorry but fuck, I was caught slipping."

"Yeah yeah."

"Damn! What a mutha fucka have to do?" He asked looking sad.

"You need to get your ass up and go get a check-up!"

"Where am I supposed to go get that at?"

"I don't know. Call your doctor. Call a clinic. Shit, I don't fucking know but go get that done or you will never know how this feel again!" I spat walking away.

"You act like a mutha fucka got something!"

"Do you honestly know if you do?" I asked screwing up my face.

"Tiana, I will prove it to you. I didn't fuck her."

"No, prove it to yourself!" I said closing the door to my bedroom.

When I entered the bedroom, I couldn't see Anna, but I heard her in my walk-in closet. She already had a teal colored baby doll dress on the bed with matching accessories. This girl was getting me together like a professional stylist. I wondered what she was doing in the closet.

"Anna are you alright in there?" I asked giggling. My closet was full with clothes that I had yet to wear; not to mention the two hundred plus pair of heels I had in there. I am also a sneaker head. I had a huge collection of shoes ranging from Adidas, Nikes, LeBron's, and canvas shoes. I was still a tomboy deep down inside.

"I'm trying to find a nice pair of heels to go with that dress," she answered.

"Good luck," I giggled.

"Exactly. You know that I could organize your closet for you?"

"Really! You really can do that?" I asked excitedly.

"Yes. I use to do it back in college for rich women around Dublin and Westerville. It was fun for me, plus I got paid generously for it."

"Well, I will pay you for you to do mine."

"No T. I couldn't charge you." Anna said looking at me like she was confused.

"Anna, everything cost baby. One day you will realize that," I said pulling the T-shirt off of my head and walking towards the shower.

"I should have waited to take my shower," Anna added.

"You're cute."

I confidentially walked up to Anna and a placed a passionate kiss on her lips. Anna sucked on my bottom lip like she was sucking on my clit and it had me losing my mind. She caressed my hips gently moving both of her hands to my ass. My ass was her toy, but her entire body will soon be mine if she knew it or not. We separated and gave each other a seductive look. Before I stepped into the shower I blew her a kiss. She continued to watch me wash up looking at me through the glass doors until the glass was filled with steam.

I rushed to wash myself with hopes of getting out of the shower and taking our kisses to another level. My sex levels were high from all of the exposure, but unable to really go all in with it. I was attracted to this woman strongly and I wanted to give her a preview of things to come in Vegas.

Climbing out of the shower, I rapidly walked out of the bathroom and into my closet. I thought that she would be waiting for me where I left her but she wasn't. I did notice a stack of heel boxes from their original place. I stepped out from the closet and their she was sitting on the bed talking to Brian. I was standing in the middle of the room ready for her to take me, but I was not about to give him a show after what he did. I know his mind was racing with multiple fantasies of us having sex, but he didn't have a taste of reality. He wasn't going to get any of me or her. I went to my dresser and quickly slid on my panties. I was ignoring the two of them as they both were looking at me and giving me compliments. Anna was ready like I wanted her to be, but she wasn't catching the attitude I was giving Brian. She was just thinking of sliding her tongue between my lips.

The idea I had of having sex with her while my husband was in the dog house flew out the window. He had spoiled it when he had entered the room. I believed he was more trying to throw some shade than really trying to fuck any one of us. So, I dressed myself and was ready to get the fuck out of his sight. When I pulled my dress over my shoulders, Brian jumped up from the bed and assisted me with the back zipper.

"She's cute," he whispered in my ear that was away from her.

"Um-hum," I responded underneath my breath.

"See you later," I said turning to him. I gave him a quick kiss and grabbed my purse along with Anna's wrist.

After getting my bag with the drugs and cash, we went into the garage. I chose to drive his red Maserati today. I pulled her all of the way to the car door racing to get off the property before he could object to my car selection.

We climbed into the car and drove off. I didn't hesitate to tell her that I had some business to handle before we could do our girl thing. She nodded her head like she understood, but I knew that she didn't. I couldn't keep her in the dark about the business I had to handle in Dayton. So, I told her what I was prepared to do. I studied her face as I told her about the drugs that I had in the trunk of my car that I was going to sell. She didn't look scared or nervous at all. I would have thought that she would have flipped her wig. Anna was willing to do whatever I had in mind. I softened up the conversation with the idea of us visiting my mother and Raymond after I had taken care of business. She was with it and sat back and chilled. We hit the highway taking interstate 70 west for my roots.

Before we reached the city limits, I made several calls to local dealers in Dayton that I either known myself from school or the streets to get rid of the work. The first two calls were low level dealers that I knew would only dream of getting this amount of dope for the price I was pitching, but as I thought before I even made the call. Them fools were broke. They both asked me to front them with the food so that they could eat, but I wasn't on it. I wasn't going to be chasing no man down for my money and I wasn't going to wait by the phone for my money. I wanted to get rid of the shit today. I wasn't getting back on the highway risking my freedom again for some dope. That wasn't my life. I ended my calls with those fools and called a dealer that use to work with my brother. He was solid. He had bricks on deck. He had money. And he knew me. He knew that I wasn't going to ever try to rob him, but he knew that I was serious about my business. He was happy to hear from me because I hadn't been in the city to show my face like that. When I came to Dayton, it was to see my mother and that was it. He wanted to meet me out by the mall to do the transaction and I thought that that was a good idea because Anna and I wanted to do some shopping and pamper ourselves. I gave him the time to meet and he agreed.

Anna and I went to my mother's soon after I ended my call. I was so excited to see my son. It felt like I hadn't seen him in years, but it had only been a few days. He knew that I was coming, but he didn't know what time. I wanted to surprise him and my mother with my presence.

When we arrived in front of my mother's house, I noticed Raymond out front spraying other kids in the neighborhood with water guns. It was a hot humid day, so I didn't trip on my mother for allowing him to play with guns. She knew where I stood with that. It was bad enough that every male figure Raymond knew was either dead or locked up besides Brian. Brian was the male figure that every woman would want for her son but every time I would send my son to my mother's, he would pick up some bad habit that I was working hard for him to never receive.

THE STREETS CALL ME TREASURE 2

My mom sat on the porch with a friend sipping on some chilled lemonade. The pitcher was filled with ice and cut lemons. Although I was about twenty feet away, I could see the pitcher sweating with beads of water from the chilled glass. My taste buds begged for the cold sour but sweet taste of lemonade. Mom knew what she was doing with that lemonade. She must have read my mind and poured a tall glass as I walked toward her. Raymond finally saw me. He was running from the side of the house chasing a kid. He dropped his gun immediately knowing that I didn't approve. He stood there with his eyes on the ground. He looked like he was caught with his hand in the cookie jar. I smiled to brighten his mood and he ran to me. I gave him a huge hug and kiss.

"I miss you Ray!"

"I miss you too mom."

"You know mommy has a party planned for Brian so after that we will be back to get you."

"I know."

"You're such a good kid."

"Mom is it okay if I play?" Raymond asked.

"Yes, go play with your friends, but try to stay where granny can see you."

"Okay," Raymond said running off.

Anna caught Raymond before he could get away with his buddies. She picked him up off of his feet and gave him a hug. Raymond had a little crush on Anna and other instructors at the studio; but Anna was his favorite. He couldn't resist from laughing as she tickled him. Raymond jumped out of her arms and sprayed her chest with the water gun. I busted out laughing at the look on Anna's face. She wasn't expecting to be a part of a water fight. Her blouse was soaking wet. Her bra was revealed along with her erect nipples. Anna didn't act like a girly girl; she ran off to find the nearest water gun and joined the war. My mom and I rushed back to the porch and watched as everyone went on a warpath.

After a few minutes of chasing down little kids and spraying them down with cold water, Anna was all done with the war. She was drenched and looked cold as hell in this 92-degree weather. Luckily she managed not to get her hair that wet. My mother, her friend and I laughed looking at Anna's soaked body. I invited her inside to dry off. My mom reminded me that she had some of my old clothes from when I stayed here during breaks from college.

I took Anna into my old bedroom which was upstairs away from the other rooms. My mom converted her attic into a bedroom so that I could continue to feel like a young adult with a little privacy.

I opened the door to the room and memories began to fill my head of my good ole college days. Brandi and I used to get high smoking weed, watching 106 & Park. She would invite guys over; we would just sit, smoke up their weed, and whisper about them not getting any. We had a lot of good memories in here. Sad she's not here with me now.

Anna shuffled her feet into the room looking cold as fuck. Her lips were becoming a dark purple shade. The central air wasn't helping. My mom had the air on frost mode. I told her to have a seat and I would be right back.

I rushed back down the stairs to get her a towel to dry off. Before I could run back up the stairs, my mom stopped me in the hall asking about the trip. I gave her the run down and thanked her for keeping Raymond for me. She didn't mind having her grandson, in fact she loved having him here. He kept her alive. My mom was just worried about her little girl. She wanted to know when I was leaving and when I would be back.

When I got back upstairs, Anna had already pulled out my old Central State T-shirt and slid into it. She couldn't wait to get out of those wet clothes. Her ass was hanging out but it didn't bother me. I started picking up her wet clothes from the floor and she stepped to me and asked me to relax. Anna looked at me like she was speaking to me telepathically. I wondered; was she thinking about fucking right here and now? And if she was, I would be game. She was damn near naked and I could quickly strip down to match. She was curious to know who was the girl in the pictures that I had in a collage on my wall. I walked over to the picture frame and took it away from the wall.

Looking at the pictures of Brandi and I, my mind began to flood with multiple memories of our childhood and kicking it days. The pictures were causing my feelings to go all over the place. Anna sat quietly and looked over the pictures with me. Some pictures made me cry and some made me laugh. Not until now, I really had a chance to think about Brandi. She was my best friend. We grew up together and was raised like we were sisters. I fought her battles and she fought mine. We ate together. We played together. We shared each other's dreams. Then we shared my husband. That thought crossed my mind and quickly dried up my tears. Although we shared a lot of good memories, the bad outweighed the good. While I was deep in thought about the last time I saw Brandi's lifeless body being carried out by the coroner, I felt Anna's hand smoothly glide across my thigh. I woke up from being deep in thought, turned to her and smiled. Anna smiled back giving me a kiss.

    I gently pushed Anna back on the bed and climbed on top of her. She continued to smile with anticipation of what was to come. We kissed each other as we both smiled and giggled. I eased my hands up her side to lift the shirt over her breasts. Her nipples were hard and erect. I sat up just enough to get a good view of her beautifully toned midsection. My eyes then scrolled up to her breasts. I placed a hand on each of them as if I was a plastic surgeon looking to do some work. In fact, I was. I studied each breast wrecking my brain on which to have first. I elected the left breast just because I liked how full it looked in the palm of my hand. I squeezed her breast gently and placed her nipple into my mouth. I sucked and licked on her breast passionately. Anna purred like a cat enjoying the touch of my soft lips on her breast. After sucking and twirling my tongue over her left breast, I decided to give the other some attention. I pushed her breasts together since I felt as if I was neglecting the other breast and sucked them both together. She moaned as I rapidly licked her breast. With Anna's eyes closed tightly, I sat up and flicked my tongue across her lips. I felt as if I was changing into some sort of wild animal. I felt on her waist feeling the thin panty strap that hugged her waist. I playfully tugged on her panties; causing her to shift her body just enough to rip her panties off. I tossed them on the floor and went back to work. I reached my fingers between her thighs and dipped my finger into her already wet pussy. Anna's pussy was tight causing my index finger to feel onto each side of her walls. If I was a man, I would love to dive inside of this pussy. The idea alone had me wanting to put on a strap-on, but we were going to do that at a later date. Her facial expressions expressed nothing but complete ecstasy. I stopped sucking on her breasts and started kissing her torso easing my body down hers. I didn't stop kissing her body until I was in eye view of her clit. I placed my hands on the inner part of her thighs and pushed them both into the air. I parted her pussy lips with my tongue tasting her nectar. My tongue swirled over her clit swiftly causing her legs to tremble in my hands. Then the chime of my phone went off interrupting us.

Ring! Ring!

"What the fuck!" I shouted becoming annoyed.

Anna took a deep breath, "Treasure don't stop."

I didn't want to stop, but my phone wasn't going to let up either.

When I came up for air, Anna had a look of disappointment on her face. I knew that she was about to cum, but I had to answer. I picked up the phone and noticed the call was important. The caller was the dealer that I had planned to meet to sell the drugs to.

While I am discussing business, Anna started massaging my shoulders. I was a little tense from all of the drama and stress that I had been through. Her hands felt like I was at a professional massage parlor. Anna added to my pleasure planting soft kisses on the back of my neck. I was smiling from ear to ear, trying to conduct business but enjoying her touch at the same damn time.

The dealer wanted to change the plans of the meet. He wanted to meet at a car audio and rim shop on Main Street. I agreed because I was ready to get rid of the product and didn't want any further delays. I had plans with the money before I even had the cash in my hand. I just wanted to take care of business and spend some time with my girl.

When I ended the call, Anna had stopped massaging me and positioned herself for me to go back to where we had left off. I studied her pretty pussy over carefully but I knew that we didn't have much time before I had to meet the dealer. But, I didn't want to leave her hanging. I knew how that felt. Getting all aroused and you are ready to have an orgasm and don't, so I dove right back in like I left something.

After Anna came, I wanted more, but I knew better. I rushed back down stairs and threw her clothes into the dryer. As her clothes dried, I told her again what I had planned to do. Again, she claimed she understood and was ready to ride.

Soon, Anna was ready and dressed. We went back down and said our goodbyes. Raymond didn't pay me much attention because he was ready to get back to playing with his friends. That was cool.

Before I pulled off, I reached in my purse and gave my mother two thousand dollars plus an extra five hundred to put on Lamar's books. I had to hold both my mother and my brother down. My mom was only receiving a weak ass $900 check from the government a month. That couldn't pay for shit, so I helped her. Mom also loved to shop, so giving her the freedom to do a little shopping eased my mind. I wanted my mother's life to be carefree. Doing for them was like breathing to me. It was something I had to do. Besides, I know that if I were ever to be imprisoned Lamar would take care of me and Raymond.

CHAPTER 9

Anna and I pulled into the parking-lot of the rim shop. The shop didn't only sell rims and audio, but they also detailed cars. The parking-lot was full of cars. I noticed right at the corner of Main that a man was selling some barbeque. So, that brought even more people to the shop. I couldn't count how many dope boys were up here to get their cars either washed or tricked out with a new set of feet. All they wanted to do was show of their wealth for the thirsty ass chics in these streets but little did they know that there were two kinds of people watching; the cops and the robbers. Only if they knew that I was a wolf surrounded by a bunch of sheep.

Anna and I climbed out of the car feeling the sun beaming on us. I wanted to hurry and get inside before the barbeque smoke took over my cucumber melon fragrance. More importantly, I didn't want to get swarmed by a bunch of stuntin' ass men. They would be quick to rush Anna and me.

I stopped her in her tracks; remembering what I was here to do. I wasn't going to bring her around this mess. She wasn't built for this shit at all. I couldn't have it on my conscience that I was the one who put her in the game. Shit, I wasn't even in the dope game.

She didn't like the words that were coming from my mouth, but it was in her best interest. My brother always told me that when I went to handle business make sure that I was ready for anything that could come my way. That meant anything could happen. I could be robbed, raped, set up, shot, and I would have to handle my business. Anna couldn't do this and I wasn't going to put her in the fire.

Anna climbed back into the car and took a seat. I walked over to her side of the car and asked her to roll down the window. She stared at me with this fierce look. I felt like I did something wrong, but I wasn't going to go against my gut feeling. Again, I reminded her of what we were her for and she just continued to stare at me without changing her facial expression. I didn't have it in me to tell her to just come on in with me. I bent over sticking my head into the window and gave her a kiss on the lips.

"I'll be right back," I whispered.

She remained silent.

"Damn!" A crowd of men shouted checking out my ass and the kiss that I just planted on Anna's lips.

I looked at them like they had said something disrespectful and they saw it. A few continued to rant; asking me to share Anna with them and if they could get my number. But, I didn't pay them any mind. I just rapidly stepped toward the entrance like a New York business woman in downtown traffic.

As I approached the door, I saw the man who I was here to see. I lifted my free hand up for the door handle and he rushed for the door to open it. I squeezed by him and removed my eyeglasses from my face. We embraced for a quick second and separated. He pointed to the manager's office in the back. I allowed him to enter the room first because I knew how someone could be waiting on the other side of the door. He closed the door behind us. I noticed an older black-man sitting in a chair with a towel and tire cleaner in his hands. I wondered if the man was waiting for him to talk to him. The man's hands were filthy. He had oil and dirt smashed in his nails. He stuck his hand out for me to shake but I tried to look away. He quickly wiped them on the towel and tried again. I reluctantly accepted and shook his hand.

"This is my Uncle Ray, Treasure." the dealer said pointing at the man.

"Nice to meet you," I responded.

"He will be testing the product."

"Come on now. Since when have you heard of me cheating somebody on some dope. You know that ain't my thing," I said feeling irritated. I turned for the door and as soon as my hand touched the knob I thought about the money.

"Treasure, I don't want to come off as disrespectful, but I know how you get down. I can't afford to take a loss."

"I respect that. Let's just get this over with," I said waving for him to hurry and do his thing.

I took a seat across from the dealer's uncle and watched him stick his hand in the bag and placed a brick on the desk. "Looks good Treasure," the dealer said using a low tone of voice. The uncle took out a blade from his pocket and busted the brick open. He had about a gram of coke on the blade and snorted like it was nasal spray. "Damn unc!" The dealer laughed.

I stood back to my feet knowing that the uncle would approve the product. I smiled looking at the reaction the dope gave the man. He was clearly satisfied with the free gram he just snorted.

"Now are you ready to talk business?" I said sarcastically.

"Yeah we can talk, but let me hit my partner to see if he wants to go half with me on this shit."

"No, hold up! I'm not here to put on some sort of fucking audition for you mutha fuckas!"

"Treasure, I don't have the money in here with me. He does. He will bring the money here shortly."

"You know that's some bullshit!" I said with a lot of attitude.

"It's only business," he responded shaking his head.

"I bet you wouldn't do this if I were my brother or anybody from his crew."

He sat quietly fiddling with his fingers not responding. I didn't say another word and waited for this so called partner to enter the room. I was already adding tax to these weak ass mutha fuckas. I only wanted twenty-two a piece at first. Now I want twenty-five.

Suddenly my phone began to ring. Something told me to check to see who it is. I reached inside my purse to get my phone and both the uncle and the dealers eyes were all on me. I believed that they thought that I was going to pull out my pistol, but instead I pulled out my cell phone.

"Hello," I said, talking into the receiver.

"Treasure..." Anna said then paused.

"What?"

"I just overheard some guys out here talking about robbing you."

My heart began to pound rapidly. I turned towards the door and lowered my voice for only her ears to hear. "Are you sure?"

"Hell yeah I am sure! They are on their way inside now. I believe I saw both of them with guns on their waist."

"How many?"

"Two. What do you want me to do?"

"I want you to pull right up to the front of the door. Leave the passenger door open and keep the car in drive. No matter what you hear you wait for me," I instructed continuing to whisper.

"Okay! I got your back girl." Anna said ending the call.

I turned back facing them. I played it off like I was continuing my conversation with my husband. It came easy since I always talked dirty to Brian when he was horny. They sat listening and giggling amongst themselves. Playing with a man's mind was a special gift I held.

"My bad, that was my husband. I had to let him know what was about to go down tonight when I arrived back home."

"Damn Treasure. You are the perfect package for a mutha fucka," the dealer spoke up.

"How is that?" I questioned getting closer to him. I was giving him a sensual look like I was reading his mind and allowing him to read mine. I wanted him to think that I could show him better than I could tell him.

"You are sexy as fuck; classy, hood, smart, and know how to treat a man."

"Thank you. You mind if we chill alone until your partner arrive?" I asked using my best seductive voice that I had mastered.

"Hell nah! Unc let us have some time to talk."

"Okay talk," he said laughing as he walked out the door.

I sat on the desk continuing to look at him like I was fucking him with my eyes. I looked over the desk to make sure that he wasn't holding a pistol in his lap, but to my surprise he was holding his dick. I was really turning this man on.

I spun around on the desk like I was using the desk to perform gymnastic moves. I opened my legs so he could get a slight peek between my legs. When I found his eyes traveling from my face to between my thighs I reached inside of my bag and grabbed my gun. He leaned forward as if he wanted to taste my goodies. Quickly, I pulled the gun out and put my gun against his forehead.

"This is what we are on?" He asked sounding salty.

"Yeah mutha fucka. You thought that I wasn't on your bullshit. I know you got your partner outside of the door ready to lay me down so I called in a little back up."

"Treasure it ain't like that."

"Then what is it like?"

"I was just bringing him into play just in case…"

I cut him off. "Just in case what? What mutha fucka? Spit the shit out!"

"Just in case you were planning on robbing me!" He shouted.

"You know what, I should. I should have your ass empty out that mutha fucking safe and leave you in here broke as hell."

"Come on Treasure. Everything is cool."

"No it ain't cool mutha fucka! You wanted to set me up. You know what? Since you like to see a little skin, I want you to strip mutha fucka!" I ordered, pointing with the gun to take his clothes off.

"What?"

"You heard what I said!" I pushed him back using the heel on my shoe.

"I'm not doing that. You got me fucked up!" He spat screwing his face up.

"Unless you want to leave out of here in a body bag, you will take that shit off!" I ordered hopping off of the desk.

"Treasure, don't do me like that," he pleaded.

Boom! Boom! Someone banged on the door. "Yo!" A man's voice shouted on the other side of the door.

I forced the gun against his neck.

"Give me a minute. I'm handling some business."

"Alright!"

I didn't hesitate to help assist the dealer with taking off his clothes as I kept aim on him. He continued to mumble under his breath, but he knew what time it was. Like he said, he knew my reputation very well. He knew that I wasn't afraid to pull the trigger either. I was surprised to see that he had the balls to try me. These Dayton mutha fuckas never seem to amaze me. They didn't give a fuck who you were or who you knew. They were always looking for food. I had to respect it.

Minutes after the banging at the door, I had him totally naked. Well, I allowed him to keep his socks on. This fool was so stuck on the pussy that he managed to forget that he had a pistol on him. I snatched the .40 from his belt and forced him to pull off his pants and underwear.

"Get your ass up!" I ordered.

I grabbed him by the back of his neck and we walked towards the door.

"Treasure this is fucked up."

"No, what's fucked is the thought of my brother getting a hold of you and your bitch ass partner when he gets out. You know that mutha fucka is crazy."

"Damn, I don't know what I was thinking."

"I don't either," I managed to laugh.

"What do you think is going to happen when we get on the other side of this door?"

"If your boy value your life, he will watch you walk me to my car like a gentleman."

"That's fucked up."

"Let it be fucked up then." I aggressively pushed him against the door. "Now open the damn door."

He tried to turn the knob slowly but when he felt the barrel of my gun behind his ear, he went ahead and turned the knob opening the door. I remained behind him not allowing anybody to see that I was forcing him out until I was close to the door. I managed to look around him and towards the direction of the glass door leading to the parking-lot. I saw Anna looking in my direction with the door wide opened waiting for me.

"What the fuck is going on here?!" Uncle Ray shouted. He stood looking at his naked nephew with disbelief. "Young lady whatever he done, it doesn't mean you have to take his life. Can you please just put down the gun?"

Uncle Ray sounded like the father from the 'Meet The Klumps' movie. I struggled to keep my composure from laughing at his hilarious voice. "Uncle Ray it was nice to meet you but your nephew has to walk me to my car," I said continuing to escort him toward the door.

We walked a few more feet and three dudes, two with guns rushed us. "What's up?"

"Y'all be cool," the dealer instructed.

"That's fucked up the way you are doing my boy," one of them said.

"We are just going for a little walk," I said inching closer towards the door.

"Bitch you ain't going no fucking where!" Another gunman shouted.

"Fellas it's cool," the dealer added.

"Yeah it's cool. Now set your guns down or I will give y'all some brains to clean up in this bitch!" I spat forcing the gun to his head harder. His neck was bent to the side so much that I had a clear view of everyone in the room.

"What you want us to do family?" They asked.

"Go ahead and put your guns down," the dealer responded.

"Nephew…" Uncle Ray said not finishing his sentence.

"Look I'm not playing with you mutha fuckas!" I aggressively barked at the gunmen.

"It's just her all by herself," they said amongst themselves.

"Man don't play with her. She is serious as fuck. Put y'all mutha fuckin' guns down please!" He begged for his life.

The gunmen looked at each other then back over to us. I studied them carefully; not knowing what they had on their mind but I was ready for a shootout. Fortunately, they reluctantly did as they were told. They kneeled down and placed their guns down on the dirty concrete floor.

"Uncle Ray, can you please pick those guns up and throw them in that bucket of water over there?" I said pointing at a bucket near the main floor of the garage. The water was jet black and had trash floating at the top.

"Yes."

Uncle Ray walked over and picked up the guns and dropped both of the guns in the water as instructed.

"Now just because I don't trust you mutha fuckas, I want y'all to strip down also."

"Bitch you crazy!" They said in unison.

BOOM!

"Try me!"

All three of them rushed to strip down. I stood over them and watched like I was working intake at a prison. These guys quickly matched the dealer standing with their dicks in their hands. All three of their dicks varied in sizes, but were all nice to look at.

Again, I asked for Uncle Ray to work with me. I told him to take their clothes and dropped them in the dirty water also. His eyes were big as half dollar coins, but he ran to do what I had demanded.

When I saw Uncle Ray drop the clothes into the water, I eased my way out the door using my ass to open it. When I felt the warm air rise on my neck, I kicked the dealer hard on the ass and ran like hell to the passenger door. I didn't look back to see if he had fell or if he was chasing me. I knew that I had barely escaped with my life and I wasn't going to look back.

I climbed in slamming the door behind me. Anna didn't ask any questions and dropped the gear to drive. I sat up in my seat giving myself leverage to aim at the door just in case anyone came running out. Anna, punched the gas causing the tires to screech. We flew out of the parking-lot adding more smoke to the barbeque smoke.

THE STREETS CALL ME TREASURE 2

CHAPTER 10

Anna and I rode back to my mother's neighborhood. We parked at a park so that I could clear my mind of what had happened just over forty minutes ago. Unlike many others, Anna allowed me some time to think. I climbed out of the car and sat on the hood as I figured my next move. I knew that for certain I wasn't going to ride back to Columbus with all of this work with us. I didn't plan on spending any time in a jail cell, when I could be in Las Vegas enjoying my life with hubby and her.

Minutes after arriving at the park, I knew what I was about to do. I was going to drop the work on the other two low level dealers and take what I could. I had to train my mind to take this as a gain and not a loss. Although making some real money was all that was on my mind, I had to take what I could get and move the fuck on.

I made the call to the other dealers and asked that they both meet me at a hair shop near Third and Gettysburg. My brother and his friends ran over there a lot, so I believed that I would be in a safe area to conduct business. I planned on doing the transaction right in the public. That way I didn't have to worry about being caught off guard with somebody trying something. I couldn't put it past these two. They knew that they would not only be taking a chance with a bullet from me, but going to prison because a witness.

I continued to sit on the car while I handled business over the phone with them. They were both excited about getting some work for a cheap price and was eager to meet up. I ended my call and put on my game face.

Anna was listening to my whole conversation, so when I entered the car she just stared at me. She didn't look nervous, but she gave me that look like I was supposed to ask her something. I stared at her back until she opened her mouth.

"Treasure, I'm not letting you do this by yourself," Anna finally spoke.

"I know. You will be driving and keeping look out," I said putting a bullet in the chamber.

"No. I'm not waiting out in the car again. You had me scared as fuck. I didn't know if you were going to make it out."

"Anna you don't understand. This ain't no fucking game. The shit I do could get you killed and these fools would be quick to do it for any fucking price. I know how they get down. Any signs of weakness and they are on top of you like a lion on a gazelle."

"Treasure, I'd rather be with you when something goes down instead of waiting to find out the bad news."

"I hear you," I say brushing her off.

Anna grabbed my left arm. "No, listen. I am a big girl and I know what I am getting myself in to. You really need my help."

"We shall see."

Anna and I arrived at the hair store before the two of them. I knew that they would be arriving soon. I didn't want to draw any unwanted attention by sitting in the busy parking-lot with what seemed like every customer watching us. I decided that we would go inside the store and buy some shampoos, conditioners, and other little things to past the time. Soon as we entered, Anna catches the lady at the counter talking bad about a sister that was in the store. The cashier didn't notice that Anna was Black and Asian and surely didn't know that Anna spoke several languages. Anna's figure straight fooled the lady, but Anna took up for the sister and told the cashier off. I didn't know what she said, but I knew Anna was talking shit and showed her other side really quick. It was kind of a turn on. First, taking up for a complete stranger. Then looking good while doing it. Anna went over to the sister and told her what was up and the sister gave her a hug and left out. The sister had about three hundred dollars' worth of hair and dropped it on the floor as she made her exit. We paid for our items and made our exit soon after.

    As we approached the car, I noticed both of the dealers in the parking-lot. I placed the bag of hair products inside of the car and grabbed the bag of dope. I already had my pistol on me and my soldier on my side. So, I was prepared to handle business. I went to the back of the car and popped the trunk. I quickly remembered how easy it was for me to rob Money's bald friend. He was in the position that I was in, but being quick on my toes I had Anna hold the pistol because my hands were going to be occupied. She didn't say a word as she eased the gun into her purse continuing to hold on to it.

    I signaled for both of the dealers to come to me. They slowly crept towards us and I began to feel anxious. I just wanted to get the job done. I gave them both a friendly hug and then put on my game face. I busted open the bag and their faces glowed with excitement. They both had seen this amount before, but never dealt with it. I shot them a good price and they both looked as if they were about to throw-up. Then Anna chimed in, "How about the two of you put your money together and then split the shit?" Her idea was genius. They both only wanted to buy one and a half a piece but I can now get rid of all of it without fronting shit.

"Yeah we can do that," one spoke up.

"For all five, just give me seventy-five. That's a deal y'all can't beat. I feel like I am giving the shit away," I said pretending like it was hard for me to part ways with the dope.

"Hell yeah! Let's do it!" The other dealer said.

Both of the dealers simultaneously lifted their shirts and pulled out knots of cash from their draws and pockets. Anna was looking at them with a stank face. Although the money was dirty, I wasn't going to complain about it. It all spent the same way.

They rapidly counted out the stacks of cash, passed it over to me, and I did the same. While counting, I kept my eyes on their pistols and the presidents I was flipping through. Anna was watching my back and the rest of the lot. The idea of having her watch my back as I hit licks crossed my mind, but I didn't muster the thought out loud.

After counting and recounting the cash, I passed over the dope to them. They thanked me and walked toward one of their cars to equally separate the work. My job was done. I slammed the trunk closed and climbed back into the driver's seat.

Anna and I flew back up to Columbus within fifty minutes. Normally, it would have taken me a little over an hour but I pushed the speedometer passed ninety most of the way. I didn't even think about the highway patrol and a fucking ticket.

While driving, I asked Anna where she would like to go shopping. Anna was excited to go shop with me and get a few items. She didn't know what I really had in mind, but she was going to soon find out. I didn't have a problem buying a few clothes for the trip, but I was going to do some shopping for some toys that we could play nice with.

I took her to the Easton Mall. This was my favorite place to shop and it wasn't far from my house in Westerville. Easton had all of shops that I had visited often, but more importantly the mall had a lot of places to eat; no matter the budget. I always found my way into a restaurant after I did a couple hours of shopping.

Anna and I went into a few stores purchasing multiple outfits a piece. I wasn't going to buy much because I still had clothes that Brian had bought me not too long ago. I noticed that Anna was putting back clothes that I knew would look good on her and she bought things that were just okay. Nothing spoke out saying that she was going to turn up in Vegas.

Before leaving the mall, I had one last place to go in, Victoria Secret. I wanted to buy a piece of lingerie for every night that we were going to stay in Vegas. Brian was going to feel like a kid in the candy store deciding which piece of eye candy he wanted to taste first. Anna was hesitant to pick out lingerie even the pieces I suggested. It finally hit me that she might not have the money to do all of this shopping like I was accustomed to.

"Anna is there anything you like?" I asked continuing to look at this pink bra and panty set.

"I have some lingerie at the house girl that I haven't wore yet," she answered looking away from me.

"You know you are my girl and I got you."

"I know."

I stepped to her grabbing her elbow. "No, listen to me. I got you. Whatever you like, I will pay for it. As a matter of fact, here."

"What are you doing?" Anna asked smiling.

"Here you go," I said pulling out a few hundred dollar bills.

"Treasure, you don't have to do that."

"Yes I do and I want to. I can't have my boo thang wearing anything from her closet while she's on vacation with me. Now go get whatever it is you want and if that isn't enough, I will pay for it."

"Damn really!" Anna said excitedly.

"Really! Just make sure it doesn't cover up that ass."

We both laughed.

Anna was back smiling and dancing around the store looking through the clothes. It felt good seeing her happy. I loved doing things for others and this was just a small token of my appreciation for her. The girl really had my back today.

We left out of the store ringing up a total of $821. We both had our hands full with bags from various stores. We were feeling good and looking good. Men drove by shouting at us and the nice gentlemen just spoke with stares. We knew that they were looking, but we were into us.

We placed my bags in my trunk and hers in the backseat. We figured that we didn't want the headache of searching through the bags to figure out whose bag was whose. She climbed into her seat and leaned over giving me a kiss. She didn't have to say a word for me to know that she was thankful for the gifts and I felt well appreciated.

I was headed home to drop Anna off to her car and finish packing Brian's and my things. Brian never did his own packing and if he did, he would dress like he was back in the streets. That just wasn't a look of a boss. Although I loved the thuggish look; hoodies, Timbs, Nike's and jeans, a man in a suit did something to me. Brian kept his beard shaped perfectly like the rapper Rick Ross. He wore very expensive suits that I picked out and the trip wasn't going to be any different. He was going to be sexy to match two sexy women that would be on his arm.

Anna suddenly turned down the music, "Girl why did you pick out that bright ass lime green lingerie outfit for me?" Anna said waiting for my response.

"Why not? I know that ass will look good in it." I answered trying to keep from smiling because I was dead ass serious.

"I know you will look good in that pink one with the rhinestones on the crotch and bra."

"Will I?" I act surprised.

"Oh yeah! Your ass will be bouncing all over in that skimpy ass thong."

"I have an idea to make my ass look better in that thong." I replied.

"What's that?" Anna asked turning in her seat giving me her full attention.

"I want to get a tattoo with tiger stripes ripping up my thighs to my waist."

"That sounds hot! Girl, that will be so fucking sexy on you!"

"I would love to get something like that," Anna said staring out of the windshield.

"Will you do it with me?"

"Hell yeah!" Anna shouted.

"We'll do it."

"Now?"

"Yes now!"

Anna and I went to a tattoo shop on High Street near the Ohio State campus. I only heard good things about this shop. Brian had been in here a couple times to get some tats but he mainly got tattooed when he was down in Miami. Other artists on the label had been in here to get some tattoos more recently, so I was taking their advice choosing this shop to get my art work. Anna tossed up multiple ideas of what she wanted, but couldn't decide on a certain one. I started thinking about what would look good on her and multiple tattoo ideas flooded my mind. I shot her a few of my ideas but she wasn't with it. The last thing she wanted to do was allow the tattoo artists to just use her as a blank canvas.

I pulled onto the door causing a bell to chime notifying them of our presence. Anna stepped in first. She removed her glasses from her face and started walking towards the wall. The wall had hundreds of pictures of people getting tats in here. I joined her. Anna started pointing to pictures that she liked and I did the same. Then a skinny white girl came out from the back. She was on her phone but signaled for us to wait a minute. That was fine with me because inside, I was nervous. The pictures that I was looking at that had tattoos on their ass and waist had me almost ready to pull out and run to the car.

"Can I help you," the lady said ending her phone call.

"We want some tattoos today," I answered walking toward the counter.

Anna looked like she was overwhelmed with emotions. She looked excited and scared at the same damn time. I grabbed her hand and told her that it will be alright. Getting the tattoos on the ass was said to be one of the most painful places to get a tattoo besides the foot and wrist. The ass wasn't going to be a problem for me; it was getting the tattoo up my waist.

The lady asked us both what we had in mind and I explained my idea to her. She sat quietly just nodding her head and taking notes. After I told her what I wanted, it was Anna's turn. She walked back over to the wall and asked the lady if she could have something like the picture. Both, the lady and myself went over to the picture and studied what Anna was pointing at. The picture had a lady with a Puerto Rican flag on her fat ass. It was very creative, but I didn't know exactly what Anna wanted. The lady took notes and then rushed off to the back. She came out with two other men which I assumed were artists. One of them asked who was getting the stripes tattoo and I raised my hand like I was in class again.

Anna and I separated as we went into the separate rooms to get our tats. I was still in the dark with what she was actually getting. I hope that she wasn't putting a flag on her ass. She needed something that would represent her sexy side.

I stripped down while the man was putting on his gloves and getting his tools ready. He turned back around in his chair and his mouth almost fell open looking at my naked body. He asked me to turn to the side that I wanted him to work on and I did. I wanted him to put the tattoo on my left side because I had a small stretch mark on my right hip from giving birth to Raymond.

After the artists drew the tiger stipes, he placed the thin paper against my skin making sure that I liked the idea that I decided on. It looked great as I looked in the mirror. I gave him a handshake and laid down on my side. The artists turned on his tools and positioned himself to start. Anna suddenly crept in pushing the door open.

"What's wrong?" I asked.

"I can't figure out what I want." Anna replied.

"Get something that will compliment that ass."

The tattoo artists started staring at Anna's ass smiling.

"Like what Treasure? Yours is going to be sexy as fuck."

I stood up from the chair and grabbed a fist full of her ass cheeks. "Get some leopard print going down your side to your ass," I answered.

"That sounds dope! Yes, that's what I want! Thank you Treasure!" Anna shouted then shared a kiss with me before running off into the next room.

I laid back and allowed the man to work. The tattoo was intense. I held tight to the chair as he colored the stripes in. I didn't know that I was going to endure this amount of pain for this tattoo, but it was coming out like I had imagined.

THE STREETS CALL ME TREASURE 2

Two hours had passed since he first started. I was unable to relax because of the pain. But I was able to capture a photo while he was putting the stipes along my side. I wondered how many likes I would get on Instagram if I decided to post this pic.

When he finished, he helped me to my feet and allowed me to look at the art he had placed on me. I stood in front of a mirror admiring his work. The tattoo actually made my ass look a lot better and fatter but maybe because it was a little swollen from the constant sticking of the needles. I gave him a hug and thanked him for the awesome work. I promised to be back really soon.

Anna was laying on her stomach when I entered the room. Her ass was red as fuck where the man was applying the ink. I noticed the leopard tattoo going down her side but she added more to her list. Right under her ass cheeks it read, "Delicious Peach" a word under each ass cheek. The tattoo artist was adding a juicy looking peach on her left ass cheek. The peach made you want to take a bite of her ass. I guess that was the point. Super sexy though. I started taking pics of her ass like I was a photographer. Anna didn't know that I was in the room until I slipped my finger between her legs. Anna almost jumped out of her skin thinking that the finger belonged to the tattoo artist.

"What the fuck! Treasure! Anna shouted."

"What!?" I said trying to sound curious.

"I thought he was trying to put something in my cooch."

"Nah, that was me. I will definitely be putting something in there when we hit Vegas."

"I'm ready," Anna said pulling her pants over her humps.

"Well, I guess we have one more place to stop."

"What's that?"

"We have to go toy shopping."

"You are speaking my language," Anna smiled.

Anna and I left the tattoo shop and headed for a sex toy shop that was close by. We entered the shop all silly acting not knowing exactly what we wanted, but we knew that we needed a nice size dildo to fuck the both of us. We laughed about the idea of Brian trying to handle two freaks at the same damn time. Anna and I could go all night and I knew personally that Brian wasn't going to be up to par. He might last a few rounds, but we were going to knock his ass out like Tyson.

"Girl you go look over there and I will look over here. Grab whatever you like and I will meet you at the counter," I instructed.

Anna disappeared down another aisle while I was looking at the various strap-ons. I wasn't going to buy any wild shit like Money was using in his freak factory. I was looking for something that we both could use to enjoy each other's company. Images of her tasting my goodies in my office at the dance studio started to flood my head. I couldn't wait to have her tongue between my pussy lips again. I quickly grabbed a strap-on that had an 8-inch penis and anal vibrator for twice the pleasure. Right behind me were feathers and whips, but I wasn't into that type of shit. I strolled on down the aisle getting closer towards the cashier and I noticed flavored edible lubes. I grabbed all sorts of flavors including my favorite- cherry. I have used this many times on Brian. He knew that when I put this down his shaft that I was going to suck his dick for a minute. I placed everything on the counter and waited for Anna. She came to the counter with a small basket full of items. I believed that she was anticipating this trip more than I was. The cashier started ringing up the items. I was in a trance. I wasn't shocked from the price, but the toys. This girl picked anal beads, a long ass 18-inch double dildo, a blind fold, and the award winning rabbit vibrator. I couldn't help but laugh at the shit she picked out. This was going to be a wild a wild week in Vegas.

When we pulled up into my driveway, I noticed Redd and a few other artists' cars in the driveway. I wasn't expecting to see all of them today because our flight was leaving tomorrow and I needed some rest. Theses clowns stayed turned up on a daily. No matter what time of day it was, these dudes were partying. I knew that if I took her in there, they would be all over her like bees on honey. I had to put her on game.

"Anna, my husband has some artists over. They are some thirsty ass dogs. Just ignore them and walk back to my room," I instructed.

"Oh, I don't want to distract them from what they are doing."

"No. No. No. It's not you. Trust me. They are like that with any piece of pussy that comes around," I said.

"Treasure, it's fine. I will just come by in the morning to catch the flight with you guys," Anna said taking out her bags.

"Girl cut it out! You are staying here tonight. It will be easier on you and me," I interjected.

"You sure?"

"Yes. We will have a girl's night. We can watch some movies and I will order some food."

"That sounds like a damn good plan to me!" Anna said happily.

"You can also show me how that lingerie fits on you," I joke holding up the pink bag.

Anna and I walked right pass Redd and the rest of the artists who were sitting around the living room like they were shooting a music video. They had clouds of weed smoke in the air and bottles all over. I figured that they were over to kick it with Brian for his birthday since we were going to be in Vegas for his actual birthday. They all stared at me like I was about to flip my wig, but I didn't say a word. Brian sat on the loveseat blowing out clouds of smoke with a drink in his other hand. He was wearing a tank-top and a pair of cut up jeans. He looked relaxed. I allowed him to be him around his boys, but he knew that I hated them fools in my living room because they were loud and didn't have any respect for other people's shit. We paid a lot of money for the furniture and I'd be damned if one of these fools fuck up my shit just to kick it.

Anna must didn't understand the words that fell from my mouth earlier. These men were like blood hounds, sniffing around for some new pussy. Anna stopped in her tracks when Redd jumped all in her face. Redd wasn't bad looking. You could tell that he wasn't really taking the music seriously and preferred the streets over a real music career. I don't know why Brian dealt with this fool. He claimed that he was a little homie who he had mad love for, so he tried his best to keep him away from their old lifestyle. I adored Brian's love for his friends; old and new. But, he had to realize that he was a married man and his wife wasn't going to deal with the foolishness around their son or house. Anna leaned against the wall smiling listening to all of his bullshit. For a minute I stood listening to their conversation until Brian asked me to come to him. Instantly I caught an attitude because I knew that he wanted me to get away from tuning in on their conversation.

"Tiana, let's go to the room." Brian whispered smoothly. He brushed his beard across my neck as he leaned in to kiss me. I could smell the liquor and weed on his breath and it wasn't a delightful sent.

"Brian - entertain your guests and we will see," I said simply.

"We will have a little company?" Brian smiled.

"Brian relax. Don't act like these thirsty ass negroes," I said walking back towards Anna.

Redd was a dog much like my brother. I knew that he would try anything to get into Anna's panties and I wasn't going to allow that to happen. I stepped right in the middle of them and snatched her ass up.

"Damn Treasure you're going to play me like that!?" Redd shouted getting upset.

"No, you played yourself," I said as I kissed Anna on the lips in front of everybody.

The crowd of people started cheering and shouting for us to put on a show. I tried to tune them out, but their voices submerged into my thoughts as we kissed. Anna was feeling me up, but I had to stop her because I wasn't going to be used for their entertainment.

When we separated Brian was standing to his feet looking like he was ready for me to give him the word to join. But we didn't. I grabbed her by the ass and escorted her to our room and closed the door behind us.

CHAPTER 11

Last night after our huge exposure of affection for another in front of Brian and his friends, we went into my room to get away from the chaos. We could hear the music blasting outside of my bedroom door, but we ignored it and focused on entertaining each other. It didn't take us long to start after I closed the door behind us. I locked the door and when I turned around, she was giving me a strip show. Anna turned the television to the music channel and started to dance. Unlike Money's baby momma, this girl could dance her ass off. She was working her ass like we were at Club Onyx in Charlotte on CIAA weekend. While watching her, I started pulling off a piece of clothing one by one. I thought that she wanted to get straight to it, but she honestly wanted me to see what she was working with. I played along and made it rain in my room showering her ass cheeks with $20's and $50's. I can't lie, I made her work for the cash. We were having a lot of fun.

Anna put on a sweet show working her body to the beats. She danced for me for about a half hour and wasn't going to stop until I crept towards my bathroom and told her to follow me. I disappeared in the bathroom from her sight and turned on the all four body spray shower. Anna and I entered the shower together. I lathered my loofa and caressed the curves of her breasts with foam. I worked the loofa down between her legs. I washed her body like I would wash mine, but I was a bit gentler. The warm water hit her, causing the soap suds to race down her body. I took this time to spread her pussy lips apart forming the "peace sign" with my fingers. She moved away from a body spray causing it to hit me directly on the breasts and hair. My hair was getting wet and curly but I didn't mind. Anna took her right hand and grabbed a handful of my curls. This turned me on. I pressed her body against the sea green subway tile and she placed her foot on the bench inviting me out to eat. I maneuvered my tongue between her lips getting good and wet. Anna started to moan when I scrolled my tongue over her clit. Anna reached down and took my left hand to her breast. I squeezed on her breast and played with her nipples simultaneously sucking on her clit. Anna begged for me to switch positions with her, but I owed her one from my mother's house. She was squirming like crazy against the tile until her legs gave out and she took a seat on the bench. We laughed together then I went back in. I lifted her right leg up in the air and inserted two fingers inside of her. I had a clear visual of my fingers at work. Her pussy was pretty and a nice shade of pink inside.

"Damn Treasure that feels so good," Anna sensually said.

I knew that she was ready to have an orgasm. I kneeled down and swirled my tongue rapidly in a circular motion over her clit causing the leg I was holding to shake. She held my head down on her clit. "Oh shiiiit!….Oh shit!...Treasure!" Anna screamed spilling her juice into my mouth like a faucet.

Twenty minutes passed since we entered the shower and I heard a loud bang coming from my bedroom door. I almost forgot that we weren't in the house alone. Anna and I took our time getting out of the shower, but the banging didn't stop. We crept out of the shower like we were sneaking around someone else's crib. We both dried off and I had to find her something comfortable to put on. I had a variety of robes; silk, cloth, and satin. She objected to all of them.

Bang! Bang! Bang! The sound from the other side of the door.

"Tiana open the damn door!" Brian shouted.

"We are getting dressed!" I shouted back projecting my voice towards the door.

"Treasuuure…" Anna said, almost singing my name.

I turned to face her and she was on the bed massaging her clit in a circular motion.

Bang! Bang!

"Treasure open this mutha fuckin' door!" Brian shouted again.

"Wait Brian! We are almost finished!" I replied.

I lied. I wasn't in a rush to have him interrupt my company. He needed to be focusing on his own fucking company.

I crawled across the bed like a cat on a tree branch. I gave her a sensual look telling her that it was time for round two. She looked me in my eyes parting her legs further apart as I inched closer. Grabbing her hand, I took the fingers she was using to massage her clit and I slipped them into my mouth. Anna took in a deep breath and pulled me closer to her. We shared a passionate kiss while I slid my fingers inside her. When we separated our lips, Anna took my hand and placed my wet fingers in her mouth tasting herself. I couldn't hold myself together. I gently planted kisses across her collarbone working my way down to her nipple. With one nipple in my mouth, I played with the other. I flicked her nipples and caressed her breasts to her delight. Anna let out a soft moan, "Oh." I placed my fingers back inside her wetness. I worked my fingers inside her pussy causing her to act as if she was fucking my fingers. Anna was working her hips like she had a dick thrusting inside of her. Soon as she came, she flipped me over on my back and didn't hesitate to exchange the favor.

After I had an orgasm, both of us where tired as fuck and wanted to chill but the music continued to play loudly. I sat up from my relaxed position and moved her leg from across my thighs.

"Where are you going?" Anna asked sitting up.

"I'll be right back," I answered.

I tried to climb out of the bed, but Anna playfully held me down by the waist pleading for me to stay in the bed with her. I managed to wiggle away from her grasp. "Look at all of that ass girlfriend," Anna joked staring at my butt. I waved her off like she knew she had seen and touched this thang many times.

I wrapped my body with a silk robe and started for the bedroom door. I noticed in the mirror that my hair was all over the place and I didn't want Brian to believe that we did anything without him. I wouldn't hear the end of it and he would play the fuck out of it like I was strictly into women. That would lead to a big ass fight and I didn't want to ruin the moment that I was having with Anna. I quickly straightened my hair and threw on a head scarf before opening the door.

When I opened the door, my eyes danced throughout the house noticing all of the trash. His friends had left and they left us with a ton of empty bottles and blunt wrappers all over the place. I felt my blood pressure began to rise, but I quickly got myself back together. I stormed through the house until I saw him passed out in his favorite recliner. There wasn't any telling how long he had been sleep, but from the looks of it, it had been a while. I bent over and gave him a kiss. Like a cartoon character; he awakened. He reached around and grabbed my apple squeezing his finger into my skin. I loved his strong hands, but I had to remind myself that he was on punishment.

"Take care of your man!" Anna cheered standing behind me still totally naked.

"Damn Treasure! Your friend is fine!" Brian blurted out.

"What!?" I spat waiting for his response.

"I mean...Shit look at her!"

I turned back to Anna and she was making her way towards us. Her tits bounced with each step as she stepped closer to us. I couldn't even find the words to argue with him about his statement because she was built like a video vixen.

"What's that on your thighs?" Brian questioned lifting my robe.

"Anna and I went to get some tats today."

"Oh yeah? That's sexy as fuck baby!" Brian explained, examining the tattoo all around to my ass.

"Thank you."

"Here, turn around. Let me get a good look at this," Brian said turning me around.

Brian lifted my robe with one hand and gently touched my tattoo. I wanted to moisturize it again since the jelly came off when Anna and I was fooling around.

"Anna, can you bring me the medication gel from my bathroom?" I asked while continuing to be examined by my man.

"Sure!" Anna said trotting off. I was pretty sure that Brian had his eyes on her ass just as well as me.

"Damn Tiana!"

"What?" I asked waiting to hear what he was going to say.

"Your friend is cute. You think she would be down for a threesome?" Brian asked.

"I told you that I was going to bring her to Vegas with us. She is down for whatever."

"Oh yeah?"

"Yes. Now be quiet before she hears us talking about her."

"Treasure here," Anna said walking towards us.

"Anna, wifey was telling me that you got a tattoo today also," Brian said trying to sound curious.

"You want to see it?" Anna asked sounding like a dingy ass chic.

"Hell yeah I do!" Brian cheered.

Anna turned around excited to show her ass to the first man that wanted to see her new tats. Brian slowly read the tattoo, "Delicious peach."

"I have my peach right here." Brian announced.

Good answer.

"Anna let me show you what I would do to a peach," Brian added placing both of his thumbs under each ass cheek.

Brian spread my ass cheeks apart and rolled his tongue up my ass. I felt his tongue run over my asshole; which gave me chills. This was a first from him. He has kissed my ass literally many times, but never tossed my salad. Last year for our anniversary, we went back to his home in Miami. While we were down there, things got wild. He accidently stuck his dick in my ass, but I allowed it. That shit had me screaming my lungs out from the pain but at the same time, I didn't want him to stop. It was something different and now this. He is actually tossing my salad in front of this girl. I bent over, putting my hands on my knees to give him better leverage. Soon as I did, he took his tongue and slid it into my pussy. It was strange that my pussy was drenching wet from this new item that he added to our menu. Anna approached me and kissed me while Brian was doing his thing. I sucked on her tits and played with her pussy until I exploded my juice on his chin.

My pussy was still throbbing from last night and all of the attention it received. Anna took a place at the table to eat my pussy after I squirted on Brian's chin. He sat watching, but would occasionally slap Anna's ass while it was up in the air. I couldn't even get mad at him because I would've done the same damn thing. Her ass was lusciously curvy without any blemishes.

Anna and I stayed up until two in the morning watching movies on Netflix. We both had a similar taste for movies so picking them out was easy. We both loved action movies and comedies. We had watched about three movies until we passed out on the couch. Brian slept on a loveseat to himself, but looked as comfortable as usual. Drinking Ciroc all night long and watching movies was the perfect combination to make us all go to sleep. I didn't remember what the last movie was because I was so lifted.

The sound from my alarm awakened us. My alarm went off at 10 o'clock in the morning. Anna rolled over and said, "My pussy is still throbbing babe. That was a good night." I playfully pushed her feeling embarrassed.

I climbed out of the bed smelling food and I also heard some rumbling coming from the living room. I wondered if Brian jumped up and started to cook for us. He was always the romantic type to do shit like that, but also dropping the conflict we had with one another. His actions always caused me to melt. Brian was a true sweetheart and I was thinking of giving him a little surprise for his efforts. The thought of pulling his dick out and shoving it into my mouth as he cooked, raced through my mind. Besides, I had to give him a little love from all of the attention he gave me last night. I went into my bags and took out the flavored edible lubes that we bought at the sex store.

I walked out of the bedroom leaving Anna sprawled out over the bed. Anna was sleeping on her stomach showing all of her ass. I squeezed it firmly causing her to wake up. She looked at the time on her cell phone and started to get herself together. I looked at my robe that was on the floor next to the bed and decided not to put it on. I wanted to turn my husband's blood pressure up like a thermostat. The scent from the kitchen was so arousing. My stomach growled from the sweet smell of pancakes and turkey sausage. I knew that smell of pancakes from anywhere. I went around the living room through the dining room to enter into the kitchen.

"Oh shit!" I screamed quickly covering my chest. I was shocked to see that Brian had a stranger in here cooking breakfast and a maid cleaning. The chef looked me up and down and then removed his eyes from me before I went the fuck off.

"What's wrong?" Brian asked barging into the kitchen.

"You have folks running in and out the house that I don't know!" I spat, walking backwards out of the kitchen into the dining room.

Brian followed right behind me. "That's Chef Frank. I paid for him to make us breakfast and lunch before we flew out."

"Really?" I said surprised.

"Baby - I am going to make sure we start this vacation off the right way," Brian said lowering his voice and looking at me with this goofy face.

I laughed.

"Well, look what I got to start the vacation with," I said, holding up the flavored lube.

We ran off into the room and soon as I closed the door I sucked the hell out of his dick. Anna was in the shower getting fresh for the day, so it was just him and me all alone. I focused all of my attention on sucking his dick. The flavor lube added more pleasure for me to get more into sucking his dick. Brian had to brace himself against the bedroom door because I was sucking, jerking, and licking aggressively until he unloaded his white liquid onto my breasts.

CHAPTER 12

We couldn't ask for a better flight out to Vegas. We enjoyed each other's conversation the whole flight. We didn't talk about sex at all; just about what we all wanted to do while we were here in Vegas. Brian mostly wanted just to relax and hit the strip of casinos. It had been a while since he had really taken time from the music business just to focus on relaxing and me. He even promised not to answer his phone the whole trip. Little shit like that was the reasons why I fell in love with the man. He was a boss, but he was a softy when it came to Raymond and me. Anna was excited to see the bright lights and while out there, she wanted to check out all of the hype about Vegas strip clubs. Me, myself… I just wanted to enjoy the company of my man and have a little fun with Anna. Brian saw a preview of what all three of us could do together and it was enough to feed his imagination. I was going to give him the fireworks that I had promised for his birthday. Everything that I had in mind was going to be all new for him.

  The hotel provided a driver and a pair of body guards for the week. The driver was going to be on call for wherever we planned to go. The security was for Brian. He never felt comfortable if he didn't have one of his goons with him or some heat. The guards were going to be available any time we left the hotel. All I had to do was make the call and they would arrive in less than an hour. I understood Brian wanting to have his trusted friends and security to watch his back, but this week was going to be different. We were going to have fun and also get some time to relax.

The driver waiting for us, had a sign with our last names as we stood on the escalator coming down. He was an older looking black man who still had a little swag about himself. Couldn't help but notice the diamonds in his watch and ear. I thought to myself that he must be receiving some huge tips out here in the desert.

We introduced ourselves and he took our bags to the truck. The security was waiting for us at their car. Both of them were in really good shape and that caught Anna's attention. She went directly for the real dark skinned brotha with the bald head. She felt on his shoulders like she was about to give him a massage. Brian stood outside of the town-car door laughing at her and pleading for her to get in the car. Anna was full of life and couldn't wait to take the city by storm.

Riding in this blacked out Escalade, I began to feel the energy that Anna had for the city. We looked like we were important. Anna had her head out the tinted window like a puppy excited to see the world. I was taking pictures of everything that I had seen in movies. I was going to cherish this moment and really make sure that Brian have one of the most memorable birthdays ever.

We entered our hotel suite in awe. The place was luxurious. The scent from the beautiful lilies made the room so inviting. We walked further into the room and all of us took in the amazing view. The Penthouse had amazing views of the city and being so high up, I felt like we were on top of the world. The gourmet kitchen that was suited for a Blue Ribbon chef. Floor to ceiling automatic curtains were breathtaking. I noticed a game room; which had a 50-inch TV and a pool table. The room was so large that I could have invited more and we still would had been comfortable. I had to purchase a fully stocked wet bar which had all of his favorite drinks. Knowing my man, I had also requested the hotel to have every favorite fruit of his that I could think of. I told them that we would need these items when we arrived and they did their thing. My thing was the beautiful view. The city lights started to come on and the beauty shined in the sunset. Anna went straight for the bed and flipped off her heels.

"Oh, Treasure you have to get in with me. This bed is so damn soft girl," Anna said rolling over the pillow soft bed. The bed was made from Egyptian cotton. I could only imagine how she felt, it was as if she were an Egyptian queen.

"Girl - we will go to bed when that time comes," I said walking up behind Brian. He was taking a long look at the view also.

"Baby, you did your thing with this. I am so happy right now," Brian uttered continuing to look out of the floor to ceiling window.

"I did it all for you," I replied stepping in front of him and placing a soft kiss on his lips.

"I'm proud of you Tiana."

"Aw thank you babe."

"No seriously. This is special for me. I won't ever forget this."

"Brian we just got here. You have a whole week to see all of the surprises coming your way Fat Man."

"I'm sure. Just know that I appreciate it. And I love you Tiana," Brian said bending down to kiss me.

Brian and I stood kissing for a while until Anna interrupted us. "Excuse me. Are y'all going to get ready for dinner? Because I am starving in here."

"Yeah let's go," I responded.

The hotel had various restaurants to accommodate our hunger but knowing my man, he wanted to eat at the steakhouse. Brian loved a nice juicy steak with a ton of grilled shrimp. Being from Miami, he kept seafood in his diet and I enjoyed it myself. I made us some reservations and we were out of the door in minutes after I made the call.

The restaurant was nice. Most steakhouses couldn't hold a candle to this place. They had a world renowned chef and top of the line steaks for his delight. Brian couldn't wait to sink his teeth into a rib-eye steak.

When the waiter approached us, Brian was at a loss for words on what he wanted to eat when it was his turn to order. Anna and I ordered the same, grilled chicken on top of a salad. We were hungry, but we didn't want to go back home with added weight. Brian admitted that the menu had him second guessing what he wanted because the pictures looked so delicious. The waiter asked to help with a recommendation and Brian agreed to a rib eye with a loaded bake potato and salad.

Anna and I dipped off to the restroom to wash our hands and check ourselves before we ate. I hurried to wash my hands and we both applied more lip gloss to our lips before walking out of the restroom doors.

Anna walked ahead of me back toward our table but before we could reach the table, I believed that I recognized a man walking into the restroom. I could only see a quick glimpse of his face before he entered the restroom, but I knew that I knew him from somewhere.

As we ate, my mind couldn't help but try to put together the identity of the man. I barely ate my food trying to work this puzzle. "Babe you're not hungry are you?" Brian asked taking a sip from his beer bottle.

"Um...Um... I was just thinking about something." I answered.

"About what?" Brian asked waiting for my response.

"Nothing. Just forget it," I said taking a sip of wine.

"I know what she's thinking about," Anna giggled.

"Girl you are too much," I playfully said pushing Anna on her arm.

We all finished our meals, but my eyes continued to circulate the room to find the man who looked all too familiar. I tried to wait to see if he would walk by, but he never did. I couldn't get my mind off of his face, but I knew that I knew him and it wasn't a pleasant feeling.

After leaving the restaurant, Anna came up with the cleaver idea to go out dancing. I agreed because I needed to get my mind together and focus on the reason for being out here.

Anna quickly got dressed to go out, but it seemed like it wasn't fast enough for Brian. Every two to three minutes he was running in the bathroom rushing us. He was eager to get out of the hotel room and enjoy himself. I was all for it. I wouldn't dare step out looking a mess. I wanted to make sure that I was looking right for any set of eyes; male or female.

We made our way to the club and it was nuts. People seemed like they were in a zoo. I knew the dope was floating around in here somewhere, but that wasn't my problem. The club crowd was so thick that I couldn't even see the floor as we carefully stepped to the VIP section of the club.

Our table had its very own waitress and we didn't waste a moment to get our glasses full with liquor. I had to mix my Ciroc with some cranberry juice to keep from throwing up what I just ate. Anna and Brian laughed at my precaution efforts but hey, I wasn't going to be the joke of the crowd when I threw up slimy ass lettuce and chicken.

My heels were killing my feet after dancing through five or six songs. I wanted to take them off, but I had to stay looking cute. Anna remained on the dance floor which gave Brian and I some time alone.

Brian asked the waitress to bring over another bottle for us to murder before we had planned to leave. We both were already feeling the effects from the liquor. I was wishing that he would suggest leaving now, but he was having a good time.

We started talking about the atmosphere of the club and he confessed that he hadn't had this much fun in a while. He said that he was so busy with building his business and being a husband that he sort of forgotten how to have fun without trying to be responsible. Hearing his words made me realize that we didn't get out much to enjoy life because we were always working. This was something that I was going to change immediately.

Anna finally came off of the dance floor and flopped down on the cream colored sofa. She was breathing heavily like she was in desperate need of oxygen. Brian and I stared at her, waiting for her to say something. She looked at us and smiled. I couldn't help but laugh at this wild ass girl. She was truly enjoying herself out here with us.

"Come on y'all. I know y'all are in love and all, but y'all can't just sit here when the fun is out there," Anna said out of breath.

"Girl - I am done for the night," I said taking down the shot of liquor.

"Really baby?" Brian asked.

"No she ain't! She's playing hard to get Brian," Anna interjected.

Anna stood back up and started pulling on my arm pleading for me to dance with her. I had to let her down. My feet had had enough and all I wanted to do was relax in the room for the rest of the night.

Brian stood up over me, "Well if you are ready to go babe, we can go."

"It's not that. My feet are killing me," I replied.

"Treasure take them heels off and party with us. Brian, I will send your friend over here to keep you company while your wife and I go out on this dance floor," Anna cheerfully said pulling on my arm again.

"Friend!? What friend!?" I shouted over the music.

"I don't know who she is talking about," Brian responded looking puzzled. He started searching the room with me.

"I know that you're not talking about some bitch!" I aggressively said taking my heels off ready for war.

"No some dude. He was over by the bar. He said he knew Brian from Miami. He called him Bricks," Anna said looking like a kid about to get their ass whipped.

"Some dude?" Brian asked, frowning his face with confusion.

"Where is he Anna?" I asked.

"I don't know! He was by the bar trying to holla at me until I came over here."

"Brian, he knows you. Nobody calls you Bricks but those who truly knows you," I said.

"Tiana don't worry about it. It's probably somebody I know from the city," Brian said trying to hug me.

"Well you ain't here to kick it with your friends," I added giving him a crazy look.

"I'm cool. Let's just go on up to the room," Brian said taking my heels out of my hands.

Brian grabbed my hand and I grabbed Anna's. We followed right behind him leading out of the club. Away from the club's dim lights, I looked into Anna's eyes and they were glossy as fuck. I was glad that we left because she was on her way to the floor. She could barely walk to the elevator, sliding across the marble floors and laughing loudly through the halls.

When we finally reached our hotel room, we were all filling the effects of the liquor and time difference. Brian and I were mainly sleepy. We didn't have to discuss what we were about to do because our body language spoke for us. The clock read 2 AM, so it was 5 AM our time and that was my time for sleep.

Brian had to basically carry Anna to the guest room and lay her on the bed. She was no good to either of us. She needed to sleep her drunkenness off by herself. Brian walked out of the room to change out from his clothes. I looked down at Anna and she was already knocked out. Being a friend, I stripped her down to her panties and bra. Her body felt heavy as I struggled to get her under the sheets. I gave her a kiss on the cheek and walked out.

When I entered the bedroom Brian had surprised me with a room full of red rose pedals scattered over the floor and bed. Tears filled my eyes because I was at a loss for words. I covered my mouth and let the tears flow. Brian knew that he had surprised the fuck out of me. He embraced me with a strong hug and allowed me to cry on his shoulder. Moments later, Brian slowly peeled my clothes off until all I had on was my panties. He stepped back and took a seat at the foot of the bed.

"Damn you look good," Brian said licking his lips. "Here put these back on," he said handing me my heels.

I giggled feeling weird, but I did as instructed. This was his birthday week and I was going to do my job as a wife and take care of my man. Brian leaned back on the bed and took the remote that controlled everything in the room and opened the curtains. I was in shock that he wanted the curtains open, but I didn't dare argue with him. His eyes were looking down on the tablet size remote and next I heard Trey Songz "Jupiter Love" song softly play through the speakers.

"I want you to dance for me," Brian said putting his eyes back on me.

I closed my eyes and allowed the song to vibrate through my body. I started moving, fantasizing that I was on top of him in total control as I rode his dick.

The song wasn't even a minute in and I was working my body like I was at Dominican night club. I worked my hands up my waist to my breasts and caressed them to his delight. My man loved every inch of me, so I was going to show him. The liquor made me feel better and I allowed the lyrics to take over. I turned around and showed him my apple, I twerked my ass like he was making it rain on me. Brian slapped my ass and slid his finger between my pussy lips. I went over to him and gave him a lap dance. He reached around and with both of his hands he squeezed my breasts causing me to get wet between my legs. Something about this man's hands against my bare skin drove me insane. I continued to bounce and grind on his dick until the next song came on. Twister's "Wetter" was the next song and that song turned me up even more because I was actually getting wetter. I stood up continuing to dance, but I teased him with a view of my pearl. I tucked my panties between my lips and flossed my pussy. Brian bit down on his bottom lip staring at my clean shaven pussy. I cleaned it up just for him. I turned back around giving him another ass shot. I dropped down to the floor and bounced my ass off the floor like a professional stripper. He was going crazy. I looked over my shoulder and he was coming out from his clothes. I laid down on my back and spread my legs eagle holding on the heel of my shoes. Again, he sat up and rubbed his fingers over my pussy. When he removed his hand, I slowly took off my panties and threw them at him. I looked up at him and his dick was fully erect. The thickness of his dick had my pussy crying. He got up from his seat and reached down picking me up from my waist. My weight didn't matter to him nor crossed his mind. He picked me up like I was a bag of groceries. He lifted me up until I was face to face with his penis upside down. Shivers ran up my spine down to my legs like I was about to have an orgasm just from the position. He had my thighs against his ears like he was wearing earmuffs. He held my body tight to his. His forearm was pressed against my tailbone right above my ass. I almost went berserk when he parted my lips with the tip of his tongue. I had to match him, so I wrapped my fingers around his manhood and took it into my mouth. I continued to jack him off and suck his dick while he rolled his tongue over my clit. I felt like we were in competition with one another because he was eating my pussy better than he ever had before. Brian made me have two orgasms before he was ready to have his first. I felt him tense up but I didn't think he was going to drop me. I knew it was time for him to release. This action made me suck harder and faster. I kept my mouth moving over the tip of his dick; not allowing it out for air. I sucked his dick until he released all of his juice inside the back of my mouth.

CHAPTER 13

Today was Brian's birthday and we were going to make the best of it. I promised him fireworks, so fireworks he was going to get. I have yet to share Anna with him because we have been busy with each other. Brian had not had any sex but I made sure that he had gotten a nut off every night.

Last night, we all were in the shower and Anna sucked him off while I watched and played with myself. I was saving her for the grand finale. He didn't know what to think when I had told her to suck his dick in the shower. His face looked like a deer caught in head lights when she went down on him and wrapped her thick lips around his dick. Anna also allowed Brian to bust in her mouth, but it took him a while to do it. I know that she wasn't doing a job like I had been doing over the years, but I might allow her to get more training on his thick pipe.

Anna and I had been secretly planning the perfect night to have with him, but he had his mind set on going to the casino. I wanted him to do whatever it was he wanted, so I agreed and we were headed for the door. Before we walked out of the door, I told Anna that tonight was the night that everything was going down and we were going to pull all of the toys out; giving him a show to remember. My words brought a huge smile on her face. She was ready just as much as I was. I just hoped that Brian would be able to handle the both of us because we were some freaks alone but together, we were a dynamic duel. No dick could handle the power of our pussy; we thought.

The casino was live with sounds of bells ringing, people shouting, dealers talking, machines spitting out coins, and music from the entertainment. I finally felt like I was in Vegas. The bright lights had me, but this was the true feeling that people talked about when they said they went to Vegas.

We all went to the teller and I got fifty thousand switched out for chips. I gave Brian forty thousand in chips and I took the rest. He was looking at me wondering where I got this amount of cash because bills started adding up in his head.

"Brian go do your thing. We will find something to do," I said, planting a kiss on his lips.

"Are you sure?" Brian asked.

"Yes."

"I will be over there at the high roller table," Brian pointed with his ring finger. His ring and necklaces were blinging in the lights. He looked like a rap star instead of a poker player.

Anna and I went over to the bar and got a glass of champagne. We couldn't decide on what to play. All of the lights were causing me to become dizzy. I heard that folks won a lot on the slots, but I wasn't the one to sit for hours pulling a lever hoping to win. I wanted to play big and win big. I decided to play at a near-by roulette table. Before I could step towards the table, Anna was already done with her drink and wanted another.

"Damn bitch! Were you thirsty!?"

After getting Anna another drink, I made my way towards the table. She must have felt like I was mad, so she kept her mouth closed as we set at the table. I exchanged chips and placed one thousand on black. We watched the ball bounce around the wheel until it stopped and landed on red. "Shit!" I shouted. I bet five thousand on the next turn. Again, we watch the ball bounce around the wheel until it stopped. I took my eyes away for a second and another player shouted, "Yes red 12!" I wanted to slap his ass. Six thousand gone that quick. My mind told me to get my size 36 ass up but my feet didn't budge.

"Maybe you need a kiss for good luck," Anna finally spoke.

She leaned over in her seat and kissed me in front of everyone. Men were shouting and we stopped the whole game. When we separated, I opened my eyes and the group of men's eyes were all on us. Anna took the chips out from my hand and placed the remaining four thousand back on black. The wheel spun again but this time, the ball took one last bounce and landed on black. Everyone cheered for me. They were all happy because the whole table betted on black or inside on a black number. I collected my winnings and was ready to go.

I received my winnings from the cashier and walked towards the high roller section. Anna and I both were looking around for Brian, but he wasn't anywhere in sight. I thought that maybe he took a restroom break from the table or maybe went back up to our room to wait for us. I saw a large crowd gathered around where they were playing poker at. I never learned how to play poker although I have watched it many times on television. I stopped a waitress who was walking by,

"What's going on?"

"A man has a chance to win a half million dollars," she answered.

I was intrigued to watch the players play for the large pot of cash. Anna and I maneuvered our way through the crowd and right across from me, Brian sat with a mountain of chips. I watched as he waited for the cards to flip from the dealer. I didn't know about this game, but I understood his reaction. The dealer flipped the last card and the crowd erupted. Brian also cheered; pumping his fist in the air like he was Kobe. Brian won the pot and I darted over to his seat. I was so excited for him, that I showered him with kisses. Anna went with the crowd and disappeared. I knew that she was making her way back to the bar to get another drink.

Hotel security escorted Brian and me to the cashier. He asked them to keep his winnings, but I thought of a fantastic idea. "Brian how about we take the money to the room and make love on top of it?" I whispered in his ear.

"Seriously?" he said looking at me confused.

"Yes and you can have us both," I continued to whisper then I licked his ear.

"Let me get that in cash please," Brian told the teller.

We both laughed.

After Brian received his money, it was time to get Anna and get this party started. I wanted to show my man how much I wanted him to have a special birthday. Winning the cash was an added bonus to the freaky festivities I had planned. I needed to find this girl quickly. My body was begging for some attention and some good dick would do the trick. Brian finally found her sitting at a table. I didn't know if she was gambling or just found a place to have a seat.

With hotel security behind us, we walked up on Anna. She was facing us, but wasn't looking our way. She looked as if she was sharing conversation with a man who's back was facing us. Anna took a sip from her glass and noticed us coming. She waved for us to join her and we stepped closer. My stomach began to flip as we got closer. I was almost certain that I knew this man that was sitting only a few feet from me.

"Brian, here's your friend that I met at the club last night. We were just talking about you and Treasure," Anna said pointing at the man sitting on the stool.

I stopped in my tracks and allowed Brian and the security detail go ahead of me. The side view of the man's face that I saw at the restaurant jumped in my thoughts. Shit started to add up quickly. The man that I saw go into the restroom was…

"Tiana, come here baby. I want to introduce you to somebody!" Brian shouted sounding excited.

He had his arm across the man's shoulder and waved me to come with his other hand.

I took my time walking up on them. I felt like I was carrying weights on my feet. Brian basically had to pull my arm to him so that I could look into the eyes of a man that I had just crossed.

"Tiana - this my cousin Money. Money - this is my wife Tiana," Brian said introducing us.

"Hi Money," I managed to say.

"Tiana is it?" Money said trying to be funny.

"Yes Tiana," I said simply.

"He is fine. Ain't he girl?" Anna interjected tugging at my waist.

I ignored her and kept my focus on their conversation. I wanted to hear everything that they were saying, but I also had

Anna geeking in my ear. Money was fine, but she was acting like she was ready to fuck him right on the casino floor.

Brian and Money talked like they were favorite cousins. I never heard of Money or his family. I knew that Brian's grandfather had eight children and they were spread all over the country, but how coincidental was this shit?

I played things off and stood next to Brian listening to their conversation. They were talking about Brian's music career and the trip up to Cleveland.

'Cleveland.'

"Babe, did you visit your cousin while you were in Cleveland?" I asked Brian.

"Um nah baby. He was busy handling business. I haven't seen this fool in - I don't know. Maybe five years or so," Brian answered.

"It hasn't been that long. More like four years," Money said.

"Oh yeah right!" Brian replied shaking his head yes.

"Last time I saw this fool was at my bachelor party. He got so messed up that night," Money said, fixing his face like he was remembering the moment.

"Yo, Money this is my wife man. Let's keep the past in the past," Brian said sounding defensive.

"No, please continue. I want to hear about this party because I never heard of it. I do remember him saying that he was going to a family member's wedding around that time though," I requested wondering how the story was going to develop.

"It was nothing. Was it Walter?" Brian asked staring Money in his eyes.

"Nah, it was nothing. We had a good time though cuz." Money said, but quickly changing the atmosphere.

"What are you here to do?" Brian asked stepping away like he was ready to leave.

"Shit, I am here to get lucky. I was hoping to hit big like you."

"It was luck cuz."

"You are a lucky mutha fucka - ain't you?"

Brian laughed. "Are you staying here at the hotel?"

"Yeah. I am in room 1024."

Anna quickly put his room number in her mental rolodex. I did as well. I was going to find a way to get to his room one way or another.

"Well we will link up tomorrow before we get ready to fly out."

"Today is your birthday right?" Money asked knowing.

"You don't forget shit do you?" Brian asked.

"Nah, I don't forget shit!" Money said aggressively looking directly at Brian.

When Brian turned to walk away, Money took his eyes off of Brian and put them on me. I knew then that he knew that I had robbed him. I couldn't figure out how he knew where I was. I didn't tell his stupid ass baby momma. He was here for something and I had to figure it out soon.

Brian, Anna, the two security guards and myself made our way to the elevator. Anna couldn't wait to get to the room. She started rubbing my hips working her hands down to my ass. The security guards tried to remain professional, but I knew they were watching. We kissed and felt on each other like we were the only ones in the elevator. I pressed her body against the elevator wall and snuck my hands down her pants. I placed my hands on her ass and squeezed it with both hands. She wasn't satisfied with that and took my right hand off her ass and moved it to her pussy. I knew that she wanted me to sink my fingers inside of her, so I did. Anna let out a soft moan that was so sensual that it turned me on immediately.

Ding!

We reached our floor and we were still in the back making out.

"Ladies are y'all going to join me?" Brian asked.

We exited the elevator and rapidly walked to our suite. I opened the door and soon as we stepped foot inside we were tearing our clothes off. Brian entered last with the bag full of money. He stood near the door frozen looking at two curvy naked women. I nodded for her to help me get his clothes off also. We ran towards Brian attacking him. Anna and I quickly undressed Brian getting him down to nothing but the chains on his neck. I felt Brian up and his manhood became fully erect.

"I want you to suck his dick until he is ready to get some of this wet pussy," I said sliding my fingers inside of her pussy.

"I'll do whatever you want me to do Treasure," Anna said dropping to her knees.

Anna flipped her hair back and went straight to it. She lifted his shaft and went under it like she was taking a drink from a water fountain. Her tongue moved swiftly down his shaft to his balls. Anna played with his balls with her tongue before making her way back up to the tip of his dick.

While she had him occupied, I rushed off to the bedroom and grabbed the bag full of toys. I took out both of our lingerie outfits for the night and laid them across the bed. There wasn't any need to put them on now since we both were in the nude. Before walking out of the room, I noticed the strap-on and I decided to save that for later also. That was going to be a part of the grand finale. I was hoping that Brian approved of me wearing it, but who could turn down to freaky ass women that was ready to put on a show for a man?

When I entered back into the living room, Anna was still bobbing her head up and down on his shaft. I placed the toys out on the pool table and climbed on it. I took the pool stick and was moving it between my legs teasing Brian. Although he was getting head his eyes were on me. I opened my legs giving him a direct sight of what was to come. I took the rabbit vibrator and put it to work. The rabbit was hopping all over my clit, but I wanted the real thing.

"Anna come here," I said continuing to play with vibrator.

Anna left Brian and took control of the vibrator placing it exactly where I wanted it. Brian came over too and was sliding his fingers into her sweet nectar. He started slapping his dick on her ass cheeks and sneaking the tip on her lips. Anna acted like she didn't mind and was basically calling for him to enter her.

"Brian - let me see what she tastes like," I said watching him try to ease it in.

THE STREETS CALL ME TREASURE 2

Brian walked over to me after dipping his stick in her a couple of times. I took hold onto his shaft and sucked it while I was getting pleased. I placed my hands on Brian's ass and forced him to fuck me in the mouth. At this angle I was able to deep throat his dick and he enjoyed that. I had his balls slapping me in the face, but that wasn't any bother. I wanted him to have an orgasm in which he did.

Anna and I stood in front of the king sized bed and started kissing again. We climbed in the bed and I pretended to fuck her from the back. She was liking that shit. I decided that now was the time to get the strap on and put on a show for my husband. I reached down on my side where I was sleeping and picked it up. Anna gave me a strange look. She was actually excited for me to put it on. I strapped on the toy and turned on the vibrator for my ass to get pleased. I grabbed her by the waist and thrusted inside her. Brian was quietly watching drinking from the bottle of Ciroc.

After I fucked the shit out of Anna, I turned my attention to Brian. His manhood was half erect and I had to do something about it. It had been a long time since I had him inside of me. I ripped the strap-on off and threw it on the floor. I waved for him to get in the bed with us and Anna assisted. I pushed her down on the bed and forcefully spread her legs apart. Brian was standing behind me so I twerked my ass on his dick until I was satisfied with the length. Brian only needed about ten minutes of time to himself and he was back ready.

With my head between Anna's thighs Brian rapidly thrusted into my tight pussy. I thought that maybe he would ease inside of me and take his time, but he was happy to get back inside of me. With each thrust I threw my ass back at him causing it to bounce of his thighs. I wasn't doing my best with Anna's goodie box because Brian was hitting my g-spot perfectly. I was more focused on getting me some good dick than eating some good pussy.

"Yes…Yes…Yes," Anna said between breaths.

Suddenly all of her juice started squirting out and I made sure I tasted every drop. I wasn't selfish and I had to share, but first I was going to get mines on this dick. I continued to work my ass against him as if I was dancing on it. Brian slapped and pulled my hair which he knew was my shit. That caused me to throw my ass back at him faster than he could thrust inside me. I came right on his dick, but I knew that he didn't.

"Anna let's switch spots," I said running away from the dick.

Before Anna sat up, I had given him a condom and her some edible lube. Anna looked at me making sure that it was alright with me to fuck my man and I just nodded giving her permission. Anna sat up and snatched the condom from his hand. Brian looked nervous. She ripped it opened and placed it on the tip of his dick. Anna went down on his dick and skillfully rolled it down to the base of his penis without gagging once. Both of us looked at each other surprised to see this crazy trick. Her actions turned me on. I spread my legs apart and she dove in. Brian and I stared at each other the whole time until we all fucked into a sensual ecstasy.

I woke up out of a dead sleep. My head rested on Brian's chest. I picked myself up and noticed that Anna wasn't in the bed with us. I wondered if she was in the guest room or maybe in the living room watching a little television. I climbed out of the bed carefully making sure that I didn't wake Brian. When I got to my feet, dollar bills were falling off of my body. I don't know how much money I stepped on just to walk out of the room.

I entered the first of two guest rooms and there wasn't any sign of Anna. I peeked my head inside of the other and notice her bags opened; indicating that she quickly changed into some clothes and left. I became furious. I rapidly walked to the living room and she wasn't there. Where could she be?

Money!

I was almost positive that she crept down to his room. My mind replayed him saying his room number.

I quickly got dressed and ran out of the door. I didn't know what I was going to do without my pistol, but I wasn't going to take a lost like that from anyone.

CHAPTER 14

Bang! Bang! Bang! I knocked on Money's room door. I placed my ear against the door before I knocked and I heard Money's voice. Sounded like he was on the phone or talking to someone. Maybe Anna wasn't even here?

"Treasure is that you?" Money said trying to be funny.

I could hear him laughing as he came closer to the door.

He opened the door slowly with this smile on his face. "Money this ain't a fucking game!" I said aggressively meaning every word.

"Damn, where are your manners? No hi, hello, what up? You are rude ass fuck - you thieving bitch!" Money spat back.

Money walked away from the door leaving it wide open for me to enter. I slammed the door behind me taking out my aggression on the door. Money turned and looked at me like I had lost my damn mind. I followed him into the main bedroom and there Anna laid on the bed hog tied with tape across her mouth. Suddenly, the bathroom door opened and his bald headed partner stood looking me up and down. I knew that he believed that I was the one who knocked him on top of his head.

"Money, I can't let you do this." I said sounding like I was about to cry.

"This is the game. You know the rules to this shit. How the fuck you did you think that you were going to rob the robber? My punk ass cousin should have gave you more intel on me before you thought you was going to just get me," Money philosophized.

"What!? This don't have anything to do with Brian," I replied, becoming frustrated. How could I get my husband involved in this shit?

"He has a lot to do with this! You are really mutha fuckin' lost! Do you remember how we met?" Money said knocking a Hennessy bottle to the floor.

"Yeah at the jewelers," I answered.

"You think that was a coincidental?"

"Umm…" I couldn't form the words to speak. My mind was racing with all of the memories that I had of Money. I tried to figure out how did I fuck up with this lick.

"I found you. I asked around and watched you until I decided to make my move. When you thought you were plotting on me, I was plotting on you. I didn't believe that you were going to rob me, but it is what it is." Money said rubbing his hands together.

"What the fuck?"

"Yeah we are two of the same shorty. I am just a couple of moves ahead of you. This game we play ain't checkers - it's chess. You've just been checked mate."

I took a deep breath trying to make sure my next move was my best move. I couldn't believe how well this man did his homework on me. It was sort of flattering in a strange way.

"Money…"

He cut me off in mid-sentence.

"Save that shit! You know that man you call your husband has tried to keep you from our family because he did some fucked up shit to me?"

I processed his words and it was true. I only met his mother twice and that was once we were in Miami and once at the wedding. He did keep them from me although I wanted them involved with everything we had going on.

"What did he do?" I inquired, truly wanting to know.

"Well the night of my bachelor party, your husband left early and went to go see my wife. Again, while he was up here."

"Shaniqua!? I don't believe you."

"Yes. They were fucking behind my back the whole time. So when I heard he had gotten married and moved up to Ohio, I had to get his ass back."

"That was just a few years ago," I said doing the math.

"Now you are paying attention!" Money said with excitement.

"Hold up! This isn't making any sense. How do you know that she was at his hotel room?" I questioned knowingly. Memories of the condom jumped into my mind. Seeing the condom in her purse. The lotion scent that was on his draws.

"I took her!"

"Did you?" I said almost giving up that I knew.

"Look - after I found out that she fucked my cousin, I left her all of the way alone. If it wasn't for my son, I wouldn't even deal with her ass. But, I take care of my seed."

"I know that you might hate her guts, but why would you send her to a hotel room to get smashed again? That just don't make any sense to me, "I added sounding confused.

"After that shit happened, I took her back. Not even a year later, she cheated again with somebody else. That's when I called it quits. Lucky I did because she found out that she was HIV positive."

"Wow! That's fucked up!" I shouted covering my mouth.

"This is why I need you to help me pay his ass back. The best way to get him back was how it all started."

"This is all about revenge?" I asked, screwing up my face.

"Hell yeah! I owe that mutha fucka one and I am going to cash in tonight," Money said biting on his lip. I could see the fury in his face.

"What do you need Anna for?" I questioned.

"She's my insurance policy. I know how you get down. The streets talk Treasure. You will get her ass back after you completely take care of our problem."

"I can't kill my husband!" I spat.

"Kill him if you want. I am giving you that option. I just want the money." Money said.

"How do I know that you won't hurt her?" I asked walking over to Anna.

"You don't. But if you want to test me, just go ahead. You will find this bitch in a dumpster or a hole in the dessert. You will do what the fuck I am telling you. Besides, its for your benefit also."

"My benefit? How is that?" I questioned.

"Come on think about it. You know that he cheated on you with Shaniqua. You deserve to pay his ass back. This man not only cheated on you, but he might have possibly given you the virus and your pretty ass friend."

Money handed me a piece of paper with an address. "When you have my money, I want you to drop the bag in the trash can at this address. I will then give you your friend back," he said escorting me back towards the door. My eyes fill with tears just envisioning killing another man that I loved. My heart just couldn't take the pain anymore.

"Anna - it's going to be okay. I will get you back I promise," I said, looking over at Anna as she squirmed and mumbled underneath the scotch tape.

"It would be nice if you took his head off, but I will settle for the dough. I believe he had hurt you more than he hurt me," Money said closing the door.

This mutha fucka had me cornered. Like he said, I was in checkmate. I couldn't make any risky moves.

I went back to my suite not knowing how I was going to handle this situation. Honestly, I was hurt. I believed that he fucked Shaniqua. Everything added up perfectly. I wondered if he had transferred the virus to me. I couldn't imagine not being alive to see my son grow. Because of his cheating ass, I might be dying soon.

Inside the kitchen, I searched for something that I could kill this mutha fucka with. I was so hurt and confused. I opened all of the cabinets and found the bag of money on the shelf. Brian must have hidden it while we were sleep. I jumped up and pulled down the bag and made sure that it was full. The bag seemed to have the full amount inside. With my eyes, I searched for a place to hide the money just in case something went wrong. Not thinking clearly, I placed the bag inside of the refrigerator. I continued my search in the drawers. I found a sharp steak knife in the drawer and looked at it believing that it was sharp enough to get the job done.

The room was almost in complete darkness. The only light was from the moon. I looked at him one last time before I was going to end his life. I carefully watched him breath. Inhale. Exhale. I have watched him sleep many nights, but tonight was his last.

BOOM! BOOM! BOOM! The lights and sounds of fireworks started lighting up the sky. The sound awakened him so I took this opportunity to do what I had to do. I jumped on him grabbing his neck. "Treasure what are you doing!?" He screamed.

"You fucked that girl Brian," I cried.

"What girl baby?"

"Shaniquuua…"

"No I didn't. You have to believe me. Tiana please believe me," Brian pleaded.

I had the knife pressed so hard against his skin that blood started running down from the knife down to my hand. The blood freaked me out. I removed the knife from his throat and dropped it on the floor as I stepped away from Brian.

"What is going on? Who told you that?" Brian asked standing to his feet.

"Money," I answered.

"That mutha fucka! I am going to kill him!" Brian said.

"Brian - tell me the truth. That's all I am asking because if you gave me HIV I…" I couldn't continue my words because of my cries.

I fell down to the floor with my back against the bed. Brian took a seat and held me tightly against his chest. My tears wouldn't stop until my heart heard the truth.

"Listen Tiana. The night before this fool was about to get married, I had received a call from one of my trap houses. The dude who I had running the house said that I needed to come by because my family was doing tricks for dope. Shaniqua was fucking for dope and everything else. That is how we assumed she had got the disease."

"That don't explain her in your room in Cleveland," I said wiping my face.

"True enough she came by. Like I said, she wanted to fuck me but I told her to get off of me. I did slip up and allowed the bitch to suck my dick with a condom on," Brian confessed. Tears filled his eyes also. I felt that he was sorry and made a mistake, but I wasn't about to sit by this nasty mutha fucka.

"You are sick mutha fucka!"

"I didn't know that she was about to do it. She left out from the bathroom and started crying about that man taking her to court and shit. Next thing I knew, she was putting the condom on my shit and started sucking."

"I swear if you ain't the dumbest!"

"I know. I know."

"So you didn't fuck her?"

"No!"

"I swear if I have something, I am going to kill you and that bitch!"

"I will kill myself for you Tiana," Brian said trying to embrace me again, but I side stepped.

"Brian I will be back to deal with your ass later but I have some business to handle," I said walking out the room.

With the money in my hands, I rushed to catch the elevator. My heart was going a hundred miles an hour. I wouldn't know what to do if Anna was hurt because of me. I just know that Money would feel my pain and everyone else he knew including his mother.

I ran out of the hotel and climbed in the first cab that I saw. I gave the cab driver the slip of paper that had the address of my destination. He looked at the paper and said he knew that neighborhood very well, but it wasn't a place for someone like me to be. I dug in the bag and gave the man a $100 bill. He didn't say another word and drove off.

He stopped directly in front of the house. It was a ran down Spanish style house. Trash was all over the yard and right in front of us was an abandoned car. The car windows were busted out and the tires were flat. Seemed like this car had been there for years. I told the driver to wait for me while I threw something away. I climbed out of the cab making sure that I wasn't being set up or watched. I saw the trash can on the side of the house where a boarded window was. I lifted the trash lid and dropped the bag of money inside. I quickly walked back to the cab and tried to remember Money's number, but I had so much shit on my mind that it was too hard to remember. Taking a chance, I called Anna's phone and Money answered. The cab driver slowly pulled off heading back towards the hotel.

"Hello," he answered.

"I made the drop for you."

"Good girl. I didn't believe that you were going to do it. You made me lose a fifty-thousand-dollar bet to my boy. I just knew that you were going to say fuck her and ride off into the sunset with Brian. I guess you owe me."

"Money stop fucking with me man. I know that you respect the game and I did what I was told to do. Let me come pick up my girl," I said waiting for his response.

"Damn! I didn't think she had a half of a million-dollar pussy on her. I guess me and my boy will have to find out," Money laughed.

"Money please don't hurt her!" I pleaded.

The driver was being nosy listening to my whole conversation. He steadily looked into his rearview mirror watching my mouth move.

"I ain't going to hurt the bitch."

"You promise?"

"Yeah I promise," he said giggling.

"How am I going to believe that when you lied about Brian fucking your baby momma?"

"Oh about that, Shaniqua doesn't have HIV, but thanks for taking care of that little problem for us."

"That's fucked up that you will do her like that!" I said aggressively.

"Do her like what? Pay for her car, house, take care of her and my son? That bitch is living the life and all I ask of her is to set up mutha fuckas like you and Brian so I can pay for all of that shit!" Money barked.

"You mutha fucka! Where is my friend!? Tell me now!" I demanded.

"Listen, you can pick the bitch up on 17th Street near the elementary school. I am sure you will find her," Money said ending the call.

Again I told the cab driver to take me somewhere. I gave him the street and told him that I was picking somebody up near a school. He was acting nervous to make the trip so I gave him another $100.

The cab driver slowly drove up 17th but Anna wasn't anywhere in sight. I made him park under a street light for about twenty minutes. I frantically looked out of my window for any sign of her but I came up empty. I asked the cab driver to wait while I checked the back of the school and he agreed.

I climbed out of the cab and sprinkles of rain started to fall. I ran to the back of the school not slowing down my pace at all. Again I came up empty. I found a green dumpster near a rear entrance and I thought the worst. I looked at the dumpster like it was a casket. Slowly I walked across the parking-lot heading directly for the dumpster. I felt like I was walking in slow motion and the rain drops fell to the earth each step I made. I waited for a moment to see if I heard anything but silence was all to be heard. I managed to slide the metal door open and I took a long look inside. Nothing!

I felt exhausted. The rain began to drop more heavily. I ran towards the car trying to avoid becoming soaking wet. The driver must have saw me running and decided to climbed out and open the back door. I thanked him and told him to take me back to the hotel. He agreed and turned on his window wipers. The cab driver told me that while I was gone that my phone had been ringing off the hook. I checked my phone and I had five missed calls from Brian. I was sure that he was worried about me. i studied his number deciding whether to call or not. All I wanted to do was sleep and be alone. My eyes filled with tears knowing that the worst had happened to Anna. Money was going to make sure that I felt his pain. The game was over. I had too much blood on my hands. The cab driver shifted the car into drive and turned the wheel. I let out a loud cry and tears rushed down my face. I placed my face in my hands and cried like a spoiled baby.

"Miss…Excuse me miss…" The cab driver said but I ignored him continuing to sob.

Knock. Knock.

I rubbed my eyes slowly and I heard the cab driver open his door. The rain was pounding against the car like firecrackers in a barrel. The dome light above my head was lit but I was unable to see through the clouded window. I rolled the window down and tears of sadness turned into tears of joy. The figure outside of my door was Anna.

Anna was standing outside of my door in the rain. My mind didn't register quickly to open the door because my eyes were traveling up her bruised body. Anger started to fuel my blood. She was only wearing a pair of panties and a soaking wet bra. The bra only had one strap over her shoulder. Her hair was dripping like wet noodles. I climbed out of the cab and hugged her. I was so happy to see her again. I grabbed her face with both of my hands and kissed her with joy. I knew that Money had beat and possibly raped her but he had also left her out for dead. I was going to make sure that we were going to get our rematch. And this time his ass was going to be the one in checkmate.

SPECIAL THANKS

I would like to take the time to thank everyone that have supported me from day one. My books are selling like crazy because of your support. I will continue to grind and put out heat for my readers. I love what I do and love your support. Honestly your reviews, shares, purchases, push me to become a better writer daily.

I would like to thank my queen Sinka for staying up late and listening to me read her the book until I was finished. She is one of my biggest supporters.

Thank you to all of my family and friends that support me at events, book signings, social media or just tell me to keep going.

The city of Dayton has always supported me since day one but I want everyone to know that I haven't forgot. I love writing stories about our city and our state.

To all of my readers in the jails, prisons, detention centers, half-way homes and juvenile jails. Thank you. Youth Leader Ward thanks for getting those young men some literature that could change their lives.

Also From Shaunta Kenerly

Escaping The Allure of The Game Series

I Don't Trust You

Forever And A Day

Bird Flu

COMING SOON FROM KENERLY PRESENTS

GOTTA BE SHIESTY by Terrie L. Branch

THE RIGHT ONE AT THE WRONG TIME by Anitra Hill

SWEATIN AGAIN by Miss Kim

LOVE SLAVE by Anitra Hill

CASH RULES EVERYTHING AROUND ME by Nikay Rountree

CHOOSE YOUR POISON by Terrie L. Branch

THE CHEATER'S WIFE by Nikay Rountree

www.ingramcontent.com/pod-product-compliance
Lightning Source LLC
Chambersburg PA
CBHW071503040426
42444CB00008B/1478